Research Methods for Classroom Discourse

BLOOMSBURY RESEARCH METHODS FOR EDUCATION SERIES

Edited by Melanie Nind, University of Southampton, UK

The *Bloomsbury Research Methods for Education* series provides overviews of the range of sometimes interconnected and diverse methodological possibilities for researching aspects of education such as education contexts, sectors, problems or phenomena. Each volume discusses prevailing, less obvious and more innovative methods and approaches for the particular area of educational research.

More targeted than general methods textbooks, these authoritative yet accessible books are invaluable resources for students and researchers planning their research design and wanting to explore methodological possibilities to make well-informed decisions regarding their choice of methods.

Also available in the series

Research Methods for Education in the Digital Age,
  Maggi Savin-Baden and Gemma Tombs
Research Methods for Social Justice and Equity in Education,
  Liz Atkins and Vicky Duckworth
Research Methods for Pedagogy, Melanie Nind, Alicia Curtin
  and Kathy Hall
Research Methods for Understanding Professional Learning,
  Elaine Hall and Kate Wall
Place-Based Methods for Researching Schools,
  Pat Thomson and Christine Hall

Forthcoming

Research Methods for Early Childhood Education,
  Rosie Flewitt and Lynn Ang
Research Methods for Educational Dialogue, Ruth Kershner,
  Rupert Wegerif, Ayesha Ahmed and Sara Hennessy

RESEARCH METHODS FOR EDUCATION

Research Methods for Classroom Discourse

JENNI INGRAM AND VICTORIA ELLIOTT

BLOOMSBURY ACADEMIC
LONDON • NEW YORK • OXFORD • NEW DELHI • SYDNEY

BLOOMSBURY ACADEMIC
Bloomsbury Publishing Plc
50 Bedford Square, London, WC1B 3DP, UK
1385 Broadway, New York, NY 10018, USA

BLOOMSBURY, BLOOMSBURY ACADEMIC and the Diana logo
are trademarks of Bloomsbury Publishing Plc

First published in Great Britain 2020

Series design: Clare Turner

A catalogue record for this book is available from the British Library.

A catalog record for this book is available from the Library of Congress.

ISBN: HB: 978-1-3500-7265-7
            PB: 978-1-3500-7266-4
          ePDF: 978-1-3500-7268-8
         eBook: 978-1-3500-7267-1

Series: Bloomsbury Research Methods for Education

Typeset by Integra Software Services Pvt. Ltd.
Printed and bound in Great Britain

To find out more about our authors and books visit www.bloomsbury.com
and sign up for our newsletters.

CONTENTS

LIST OF FIGURES AND TABLES

Figures

Transcripts

Tables

ABOUT THE AUTHORS

Jenni Ingram PhD FIMA, Associate Professor of Education (Mathematics), University of Oxford, UK, is an experienced teacher, researcher and teacher educator in the field of mathematics education. She is currently researching mathematics classroom interaction and the associated implications for pedagogy and teacher professional development. She is a member of the Mathematics Expert Group for PISA 2021 and one of the England experts for TALIS 2018 video study, both of which are international studies focused on mathematics teaching and learning. She also works on projects involving assessment and examinations, and social justice and equity issues in teacher education. She is Fellow and Vice Principal of Linacre College.

Victoria Elliott DPhil, Associate Professor of English and Literacy Education, University of Oxford, UK, is an established researcher in the field of English education, specializing in curriculum and assessment as they relate to the teaching of literature. She was the recipient of the National Association for the Teaching of English Research Award in 2017. She is Director of Doctoral Research in the Department of Education at the University of Oxford and convenes the Qualitative Research Methods Hub which serves the university more widely. She is an experienced teacher of advanced qualitative methods and conducts research using a wide range of different qualitative approaches.

SERIES FOREWORD

The idea of the *Bloomsbury Research Methods for Education* series is to provide books that are useful to researchers wanting to think about research methods in the context of their research area, research problem or research aims. While researchers may use any methods textbook for ideas and inspiration, the onus falls on them to apply something from social science research methods to education in particular, or from education to a particular dimension of education (pedagogy, schools, the digital dimension, practitioner learning to name some examples). This application of ideas is not beyond us and has led to some great research and also to methodological development. In this series though, the books are more targeted, making them a good place to start for the student, researcher or person wanting to craft a research proposal. Each book brings together in one place the range of sometimes interconnected and often diverse methodological possibilities for researching one aspect or sector of education, one research problem or phenomenon. Thus, readers will quickly find a discussion of the methods they associate with that bit of education research they are interested in, but in addition they will find, less obvious and more innovative methods and approaches. A quick look at the opening glossary will give you an idea of the methods you will find included within each book. You can expect a discussion of those methods that is critical, authoritative *and* situated. In each text the authors use powerful examples of the methods in use in the arena with which you are concerned.

There are other features that make this series distinctive. In each of the books the authors draw on their own research and on the research of others making alternative methodological choices. In this way they address the affordances of the methods in terms of real studies; they illustrate the potential with real data. The authors also discuss the rationale behind the choice of methods and behind how researchers put them together in research designs. As readers you will get behind the scenes of published research and into the kind of methodological decision-making that you are grappling with. In each of the books you will find yourself moving between methods, theory and data; you will find theoretical concepts to think with and with which you might be able to enhance your methods. You will find that the authors develop arguments about methods rather than just describing them.

Research Methods for Classroom Discourse explores methods for investigating spoken interaction or other discourse in the classroom. Through the text that is crafted to be clear and accessible you will get to know the authors, Jenni Ingram and Victoria (Velda) Elliott, who are well respected among the teacher education community. You will value their insights as they carefully weigh various methods, examining their principles and illustrating the distinctive qualities and complexities of each. You will be drawn into their engaging discussion of how theories and methods are intertwined, and of how the methods are continually developing supported by technological and theoretical advances. This discussion is enhanced by culturally and geographically diverse case examples that are rich with the learning they offer. As an experienced researcher who is considering doing more classroom discourse research I learned a lot reading this book. I am confident that whatever level of prior knowledge you bring as a reader you will find it is informative and helpful. You will also find it respectful of the controversies and sensitivities that come with researching linguistic matters that are so integrally tied up with identity and politics. While it is eminently practical, and has a fresh quality, this book is never naive.

This book (as with any in the series) cannot be the only book you need to read to formulate, justify and implement your research methods. Other books will cover a different range or methods or more operational detail. The aim for this series, though, is to provide books that take you to the heart of the methods thinking you will want and need to do. They are books by authors who are equally passionate about their substantive topic and about research methods and they are books that will be invaluable for inspiring deep and informed methods thinking.

Melanie Nind
Series editor

ACKNOWLEDGEMENTS

We would like to thank the following people for their comments on various portions of the book and their support in the writing process: Nick Andrews, Alison Cullinane, Nicole Dingwall, Kristine Gorgen, Geraldine Hale, Beth Hore, Laura Molway, Victoria Murphy, Lesley Nelson-Addy and Paul Riser. All mistakes remain our own. Special thanks go to our husbands, Jon Ingram and Chris Aspinall, who not only read and commented on chapters, but also entertained our children and fed us while we wrote this book.

A GLOSSARY OF RESEARCH METHODS AND TERMINOLOGY

Accommodation The tendency of individuals to converge (or diverge) their speech patterns from those of the person they are talking with.

Action research A systematic approach for practitioners to understand and improve their own practice through a focus on their own practical actions and their own reflections on data about the effects of those actions. This often involves cycles of planning, implementing, recording and analysing a change in process.

Adjacency pairs A set of two utterances in which the second is functionally dependent on the first, e.g. question and answer.

Agency Broadly, the capacity of individuals to make free choices and act independently.

Assent Gaining children's agreement to participate in research; separate from formal consent.

Co-construction The joint development of ideas and knowledge with more than one person.

Collocation Words which are frequently found together ('co-located') such as 'fish and chips'.

Concordance A list of the incidences of a particular word throughout a text.

Consent When a person makes an informed agreement to take part in research or for their child to do so.

Conversation analysis (CA) A theoretical and methodological approach for studying in detail audio-/video-recorded social interaction and conversation, paying particular attention to how the conversation works in terms of structures such as turn-taking, sequences, functions for the social context. See Chapter 2.

Corpus A large database of transcripts or texts that are connected in some way. See Chapter 6 for more details.

Critical approaches Approaches which challenge the authority of those in power; drawing on critical theory such as feminism, critical race theory, post-colonialism or queer theory.

Critical discourse analysis (CDA) An approach that brings together discourse analysis with social and cultural theory to consider issues of power. Drawn mostly from the work of Foucault.

Cumulative talk Talk in which different contributions are accepted and agreed on in a non-critical way.

Deficit model A model which assumes that someone who differs from the norm has a 'deficit' that needs to be addressed. Usually used critically in educational research.

Discourse analysis (DA) Approaches that involve the analysis of written, verbal, gestural or any semiotic text.

Disputative talk Talk where there is low co-operation and high disagreement; individuals make their own conclusions.

Distributed cognition A theory of cognitive science that argues that information and knowledge are not confined to a single mind; cognition happens within a group of people sharing ideas.

Emancipatory research Research with the goal of making the lives of participants better or increasing the visibility of their stories in the world; a feminist stance.

Epistemic Relating to knowledge and the degree to which it is accepted.

Epistemology The study of knowledge; on an individual level the person's theory of knowledge and what it means to 'know'.

Ethnographic A type of research which draws on the anthropological tradition; concerned with people and their culture it uses a variety of different data collection methods.

Ethnomethodology A sociological analysis that considers how individuals use everyday conversation and gestures to construct a view of the world.

Exploratory talk Talk in which the contributions of others are listened to, challenged and built on, so the group comes to an improved understanding.

Figured world A culturally constructed, enacted world view.

Fillers Short words or phrases used to fill time in speech, such as 'like', 'to be honest', 'um', 'er'.

Foucauldian Relating to the French theorist Michel Foucault.

Hegemony Predominance (originally of an individual, party or country) over others. Socially the dominant ('normal') example in any field.

Idiolect The form of language particular to an individual.

Indexicality A word or symbol that points to or references something in the context in which it occurs, see Chapter 2.

Insider When a researcher is part of the community they are researching.

Interactional object The purpose or topic of an interaction. Or, something treated as an object by an interaction (e.g. the gender of the participants).

Intervention study In education, research which makes a change or intervention into learning and measures evaluates its effectiveness.

Keyness A term from corpus linguistics to describe words that are unique to or occur more frequently within a particular corpus in comparison to a reference corpus.

Lexical Relating to word choice and vocabulary.

Lexical bundle A frequently occurring set of three or more words that appear in a particular corpus. See Chapter 6.

Linguistic and communicative resources The resources available to an individual to carry out communication, including vocabulary, knowledge, gesture, etc.

Longitudinal Refers to a study carried out over a longer period of time, with data collection at several time intervals.

Member checking Using participants or members of their group to check the interpretation of data and represents them fairly.

Membership category analysis (MCA) A method that focuses on how the participants draw upon certain identity categories in discourse.

Methodology A theoretically coherent system of methods; the study of methods.

Micro-analysis Analysis of very small units; in linguistics, looking at the smallest difference in utterances.

Multimodality The nature of texts to make meaning from different semiotic resources, e.g. colour, image, font, sound and words.

Narrative inquiry A form of research which considers the ways in which people create narratives about and with different aspects of their lives.

Naturally occurring data Data which would exist (if possibly unrecorded) even without the researcher, e.g. talk in a classroom.

Ontology The study of being; a field of philosophy which explores the question of whether or not things really exist.

Orientation How an individual positions themselves relative to others, the conversation or many other things.

Pace The (varying) speed of talk.

Paralinguistic features Features which are outside the words themselves, such as pace, pitch and gesture.

Participant observation A research method by which a researcher observes while taking an active part in events.

Participation rights The rights of individuals to take a turn in conversation.

Participatory methods A research process that involves the participants or those implicated in the research in the decision-making and activity of the research.

Passive voice The grammatical construction by which the semantic object becomes the grammatical subject of the verb, i.e. 'the dog bit the man' becomes 'the man was bitten'. The agent (the dog) can therefore be obscured.

Photovoice A method where participants are asked to take photos of their lives in relation to the topic of interest.

Pitch The degree of highness or lowness of tone in speaking and the changes within it.

Qualitative Research which, broadly speaking, uses non-numerical data. It is often associated with interpretivism and involves the consideration of the context in which the data was generated in the analysis.

Quantitative Research which, broadly speaking, uses numerical data. It is often associated with positivism and generally involves statistical methods.

Reflexivity Within ethnomethodology this refers to the bi-directional relationship between what is being considered and its wider effects (see Chapter 2). More widely it refers to the bi-directional relationship between the researcher and their research.

Register The variety of ways someone uses language for a particular purpose or in a specific context.

Repair A speech act which acts on trouble in a conversation to 'repair' it; for example, rephrasing if the first utterance was unclear.

Rubric A set of instructions for scoring a piece of text.

Schema theory The organization of knowledge into units or schemata.

Semiotic Refers to the meaning value of a sign or symbol or other meaning-making item.

Sociocultural A field of research which combines social and cultural factors, ultimately drawing on the work of Russian theorist Lev Vygotsky.

Sociolect A language form specific to a group of people linked by social class.

Sociolinguistic A branch of linguistics which considers the effect of social factors on language.

Stylistic analysis A linguistic analysis which draws on rhetorical and literary analysis of text rather than purely grammatical or lexical.

Syntactical Relating to syntax, which is the system of rules which govern how words can be put together to make meaning.

Systemic Functional Linguistics A branch of linguistics founded by Halliday, which considers language through the lens of choices which have been made in its production.

Talk-in-interaction Real talk within the context in which it is spoken.

TeachMeet An informal meeting where teachers share good practice, ideas and reflections.

Timelines A method where participants are asked to indicate on a timeline critical incidents in their lives.

Triangulation The use of multiple data sources to corroborate or contrast and to develop a better understanding of the topic.

Trouble in interaction Any difficulty in a conversation, e.g. misunderstanding or rudeness.

Turn-taking The structure of conversation which governs who can speak when.

Utterance A unit to describe a turn at speaking from an individual.

Verbatim Transcribing word-for-word.

Washback The effect of assessment (for example) on classroom practice, 'washing back' into pedagogy.

CHAPTER ONE

Introduction

Communication is at the heart of our existence as social beings, and classrooms are no exception to this. Through communication things are achieved; ideas are shared, challenged and debated; knowledge evolves and develops; and we accomplish teaching and learning. Classroom discourse has a variety of forms, which are variously emphasized by different approaches to research, but each of which is important in one context or another. Classroom discourse research is evolving rapidly, as it contributes to our understanding and conceptualization of pedagogy, teaching and learning, and the social contexts of learners and learning. Engaging in research in classroom discourse enables researchers to consider fundamental issues to teaching and learning, grounded in close analysis of evidence.

We will introduce a range of ideas, concepts and theoretical and methodological approaches that may be of use to the researcher interested in classroom discourse. In doing so we will identify the choices and decisions involved from the very beginning of conceptualizing and conducting research, and urge you to consider the implications that these decisions may have for your research design and for the claims which you can make from your research. This book is for you if you are a teacher-researcher, a research student or an experienced researcher turning to research in classroom discourse or interested in the possibilities it provides.

Historically, classroom discourse research began initially as an attempt to find an effective way to evaluate classroom teaching (e.g. Flander's Interaction Analysis Categories [Flanders 1960]). As the foci and needs of researchers have evolved and shifted, a wide range of theoretical and methodological approaches from other fields, such as psychology, sociology and linguistics, have been appropriated. As Edwards and Westgate (1994) emphasize, it is crucial that we recognize the relationship between the theoretical approach to researching classroom discourse and how we collect, transcribe, code, analyse and interpret the discourse we are researching. It is these relationships that we have sought to highlight in this book.

There are a number of highly influential researchers whose work needs mentioning in any outline of classroom discourse research. Cazden's (1988) was a foundational work which described both ways of researching classroom discourse and the social and cultural consequences of particular discourses on learners. Gee's work on Discourses (1999) had a huge influence on how researchers conceptualize and distinguish between different meanings of the word 'discourse'. Systemic functional linguistics (Halliday 1961) offered a micro-analytic approach which treated language as offering a series of choices, which has had a long-lasting effect on the way that researchers conceptualize the study and practice of discourse. One key contemporary researcher of classroom discourse is Neil Mercer, whose work has had a significant influence on classroom practice. We have only touched on his work and the work of his colleagues Lyn Dawes, Karen Littleton and Rupert Wegerif briefly because a more comprehensive account will be found in another book which is forthcoming in this series (*Research Methods for Classroom Dialogue*).

A classic example of classroom discourse research is one with which most teachers are familiar: the Initiation-Response-Evaluation/Feedback (IRE/IRF) pattern described by Mehan (1979) and Sinclair and Coulthard (1975). This is one of the oldest and most common patterns in teaching-learning discourses – both in the context of classrooms and in parent–child interactions. The identification and description of this pattern led to a wealth of research looking at both the nature and content of each of the moves (Initiation, Response and Feedback), and the consequences of these on students and teachers (e.g. Michaels and O'Connor 2015 and Chapter 9 of this volume).

Throughout this book we refer to the learners in the classroom as 'students'. While we could have used the words 'learner' or 'pupil', researchers interested in classroom interaction may be interested in the learning of the teachers involved, so the teachers are also 'learners'. In addition, classrooms can include students of all ages, from the very young kindergarten student to adult learners in a range of settings. This book draws from studies of classroom discourse covering a wide range of students, contexts and curriculum areas and so we have felt it most consistent to use 'students' throughout when referring to those who would generally be considered to be the learners in the classroom. Although the learning of teachers may be described, we continue to refer to them as teachers throughout the book.

There are a diverse range of theories, methods and analytic strategies for researching classroom discourse and we have been necessarily selective with what we are including in this book. This diversity is both helpful and makes the study of classroom interaction full of complex decisions. The complexity of classroom interaction means that no one approach will be sufficient to tell us everything we want or need to know. However, each approach will illuminate some aspects and give us insight into different features.

Our interest in classroom discourse comes from our own experiences as classroom teachers, and our current roles as teacher educators and researchers. As teachers we regularly engaged in a variety of types of interaction and communication which led us to appreciate the diversity and complexity of linguistic operations happening in classrooms and the different impacts these have on different students. Many of the teachers described in the case examples in this book were engaged in classroom discourse research as a way to improve their own teaching and learning, and we too have seen the value of it in this context. As teacher educators we appreciate the challenges faced by both beginning and experienced teachers in introducing or developing communicative behaviours and patterns. We also supervise a wide range of research students from a variety of backgrounds. It is in these capacities that we first appreciated the need for a book such as this which supports research students, teacher-researchers and academics supervising outside their comfort zone to access the information which they need to consider to make decisions from the earliest stages of the research process to the depths of data collection.

As researchers we come from different traditions: Jenni began in the conversation analytic tradition while Victoria as an ex-English teacher was naturally drawn to the analysis of written texts.

Through our collaborations with each other and with international colleagues our interest in and appreciation for other approaches has developed and refined. Victoria is an avid collector of research methods (going so far as to collaborate on a research project far outside her usual area simply to learn how to do Foucauldian critical discourse analysis), while Jenni is particularly interested in the theoretical underpinnings of why certain research decisions are made and how they influence the data and interpretation of that data. Our backgrounds in mathematics and English mean that we are constantly challenging each other's interpretation and approaches to language and meaning.

This leads us neatly on to the question of what 'discourse' actually means. We concur with Thornbury when he argues:

> The term *discourse* is both slippery and baggy: slippery because it eludes neat definition, and baggy because it embraces a wide range of linguistic and social phenomena. (Thornbury 2010: 270)

Almost every researcher who works with 'discourse analysis' will have their own particular conception of what discourse is. We have been inclusive in the approaches that we have described in this book (e.g. some researchers in the field of discourse analysis would exclude conversation analysis as being within it). Broadly 'discourse' can be used to describe the data which is being analysed – any spoken or written expression of meaning, interaction or other forms of interaction, such as gesture or eye gaze, or the way people dress – and it is in this way that the term is used in the title of this book. However, 'a discourse' can also be the outcome of discourse analysis. Where it is relevant we have discussed this in relation to each theoretical approach or application and have tried to delineate between what might be termed the lay and the specialist application of this word.

The book is divided into three parts. In the first we consider five different theoretical and methodological approaches to the study of classroom discourse. Part Two then develops these approaches in relation to specific applications in the context of research topics and considers how they might have different contributions to offer in the study of individual subjects. The third part is more practical, offering a series of provocations for thought that may influence the decisions you make in designing your own research. A glossary is given at the beginning of the book to offer a quick reference point to some of the terms utilized within the book.

The purpose of this series is to invite the reader to be thoughtful about methods, and we hope that this book will offer plenty of food for thought and leave you with a desire to follow up on some of the issues and choices that are raised in the various chapters. This cannot be a complete or comprehensive guide to research in classroom discourse, but we hope it will be a starting point that will enable you to make early decisions that will lead to purposeful and productive research and offer suggestions for where you can find out more.

Theoretical and Methodological Frameworks for Researching Classroom Discourse

Introduction to Part One

These five chapters introduce five different theoretical and methodological approaches to the study of discourse, with reference to the specific context of classrooms. These approaches are not exhaustive but they illustrate a range of ways in which the researcher can engage with classroom discourse, and the complexities of the possibilities. We have deliberately selected approaches which are established ways of researching classroom discourse but which are contrastive in the ways in which they approach the material.

Chapter 2 outlines the Conversation Analytic approach, alongside other ethnomethodologically informed approaches, to analysing classroom discourse. CA is one of the main approaches to research in classroom interaction. We begin with this chapter as ethnomethodological approaches are tightly guided by clear theoretical principles which underpin the nature of the research questions that can be asked, the methods of data collection and analysis, and the particular way in which these approaches interpret interaction. These approaches focus solely on interaction at the micro level. As we move through the other chapters you will see the contrast between the approaches discussed in this chapter and the others which engage in the study of a wider range of discourse and work at various analytic levels.

Chapter 3 moves the focus onto positioning theory, a relative newcomer to the field of research in classroom discourse. This continues the focus of Chapter 2 on the idea of discourse as social action but applies it specifically to the ideas around how people position themselves and position each other when they interact.

This includes positioning both within classroom interactions and within curriculum resources and textbooks. In this chapter we also consider the notion of figured worlds where the emphasis is on positioning at a more macro level than considered in Chapter 2, and which is a concept that is used widely in identity research, which is explored in Chapter 7.

Chapter 4 provides an overview of a specific form of discourse analysis aimed at the critique of power and challenging 'common sense' or assumed views of people and society: critical discourse analysis (CDA). We situate this approach within the umbrella term of discourse analysis and consider the ways in which 'discourse' is used differently in different contexts. Although there is no one authoritative way to conduct CDA, we offer one route through the research method. The individual researcher can have a substantial impact on the outcomes of a CDA and we consider issues of positionality and trustworthiness in producing useful research using this approach.

Chapter 5 explores the field of sociolinguistics and a number of different terms and concepts which are widely used within this approach to linguistic research. Sociolinguists concern themselves with the social dimension of language choices, and these dimensions are numerous. We consider some of the characteristics which might be the most relevant to the study of classroom discourse, such as regional variation, socio-economic class, gender, race, power and the sociological concept of 'face'. The chapter contextualizes these characteristics within examples taken from common classroom situations.

Chapter 6 turns to a quantitative approach to the analysis and description of language that can be used in combination with the other approaches which we have explored. We have considered how to design a corpus as well as analysing corpora and finally we also briefly consider research into the pedagogy of using corpora in language teaching. While corpus linguistics is an established field of research it is a relative newcomer to educational research and currently largely focuses on higher education.

CHAPTER TWO

Conversation Analysis and Discursive Psychology

Introduction

Within the range of theoretical approaches to analysing classroom interaction considered in this book, conversation analysis (CA) and discursive psychology (DP) are marked out particularly by their focus only on talk-in-interaction and the strong principles that researchers work with. This also leads to the use of particular data collection and analysis approaches. While CA has its roots in sociology and DP has its roots in social psychology, they draw on the same theoretical, methodological and analytical frameworks all based on ethnomethodology (Garfinkel 1967). Both focus on talk-in-interaction, that is, real talk within the context in which it is spoken, rather than talk or text in general which with other approaches are often taken out of the context in which it is used. CA has a long history within educational research and is most widely used by researchers involved in the teaching and learning of English as an additional language. DP, on the other hand, is a relative newcomer. We have brought together these two approaches in this chapter because they have the same roots and are consequently underpinned by similar principles and make use of the same methodologies but use these methodologies to address different questions or topics. DP in particular focuses specifically on those topics usually of interest to psychologists, such as knowledge, identity and attitudes and while CA also examines these topics, as well as a broader range of topics, it does so in a different way. Other approaches that have developed out of the work of CA and DP, such as critical discursive psychology (CDP), are not discussed here as they do not adhere as closely to the same ethnomethodological principles, particularly in terms of the meaning and role of context.

Both CA and DP focus on the analysis of talk-in-interaction in looking at what teachers and students say as they interact in the classroom, but also they pay careful attention to how things are said. Pauses, intonation, emphasis are all considered in the delivery of what is said, as is the sequential context in which it is said, such as what was said before and how it affects what is said next. Underpinning this is the idea of recipient design, that is, when we interact we design what we say and do for the person we are interacting with. What CA and DP researchers are interested in is how we make sense of each other when we interact through how we design our turns, but the methods we use to enable others to make sense of what we are saying and doing are also observable to researchers and are therefore available for analysis. These methods are the 'common sense methods' that are the focus of all ethnomethodological approaches; 'each "next" turn at talk will, in dealing with the previous turn, display its producer's analysis or understanding of the previous turn's content, import and relevancies' (Heritage 1986: 5, cited by te Molder and Potter 2005). What marks them out as different from other approaches to the analysis of classroom discourse is the level of detail and fine-grained nature of the analysis of what is actually said in interaction. CA and DP focus on language as action rather than language as a representation of what people are thinking. What is of interest is how teachers and students deal with issues such as explaining, argumentation, memory, thinking and understanding when they interact.

Both the approaches we examine in this chapter are underpinned by ethnomethodological principles which drive the decisions researchers make around research questions, data collection and analytic methods. Therefore, we begin this chapter by describing some of these ethnomethodological principles, and the historical context within which they developed in order to highlight the differences that result from these principles in contrast to other approaches to the analysis of classroom interactions considered in later chapters. We will also outline the methods used by researchers using CA or DP as well as exploring the types of questions these approaches are being used to explore. These discussions are necessarily brief and are intended to give you a sense of why you might use CA or DP and what this might involve. At the end of the chapter we suggest more comprehensive guides to doing CA or DP research which introduce a wider range of tools and topics.

The ethnomethodological principles and origins of CA and DP

CA and DP have their roots in ethnomethodology (Garfinkel 1967) but are also influenced by Goffman's (1981) ideas of social order and Blumer's (1969) symbolic interactionism. CA originated in the work of Harvey Sacks in the 1960s and his colleagues Emanuel Schegloff and Gail Jefferson. CA and DP are empirical and inductive approaches and both a theoretical and a methodological approach to research. This section focuses on the theoretical aspects which inform the methodology and leave focusing on methods until later in the chapter. The first studies were in sociology and looked at how people make sense of interactions through how they are organized and the shared social knowledge that we use to interpret situations and interactions we are involved in. At the time this was a radical idea as conversations and talk were widely considered to be too messy to study, and simplified, or even hypothetical, conversations were usually the focus of analysis. These structures include actions like greetings, and pairs of turns such as questions and answers, where when a greeting is uttered, that is, 'hi, how are you?' or a question is asked 'what's 2 + 2?' then there is an expectation about what will follow, such as 'fine how are you?' or '4'. These expectations arise from the structure of interactions which help us to make sense of what is going on. A key idea here is that all interactions are systematically organized, there is 'order at all points' (Hutchby and Wooffitt 1998) and we make use of this order to do particular things when we interact with others. Importantly, this order is often taken for granted in that we do not explicitly pay attention to this order in our interactions. For CA it is this structure or order that is of interest and that can tell us a great deal about how people are making sense of what is going on. Below we outline some of the key structures that have been systematically described in classrooms and are now used as tools in CA research, such as turn-taking, repair and preference organization.

The first principle is the idea of recipient design. When we interact in classrooms we are designing what we are saying for the other people involved in the interaction. Teachers design their questions and explanations for their students, but more interestingly students design their turns for both the teacher and the other students. This is most evident in the use of dietic terms such as 'that' or 'it' which only have meaning if everyone in the interaction knows what is being talked about. This is useful to us as researchers as we can see from how participants react to each other and how they have understood the interaction that came before. Furthermore, questions can be designed in different ways and these different designs can affect what the student can do in the following turn. So, CA and DP are interested in what was said, how it was said and the actions that are being done in the turn. A key driving question is 'why that now' (Schegloff and Sacks 1973: 299).

Two further, related, key ethnomethodological principles are indexicality and reflexivity. Indexicality means that everything that is said is dependent upon the context in which it is said. We can only make sense of what people are saying by considering the context in which it is said. Yet this relationship with context is also reflexive. What we say shapes the context within which we are interacting and the context shapes what we say (Seedhouse 2005). The sense of context here is on a more micro and immediate level than that used within other theoretical positions, such as those embedded in sociocultural theory.

How CA treats context is one of the main ways that it differs from the other approaches described both in this book and in this series. The argument is that we can only know which contextual features are consequential to the interaction if they are demonstrated in the actions of the participants themselves (Schegloff 1997). We might be a woman, a teacher, a vegetarian, a comic book fan and so on but that does not necessarily mean that we are speaking as a woman or as a teacher in any particular interaction. CA does not deny that different participants may be influenced by broader contextual features, such as their social status, positions of power and cultural influence, just that we cannot assume that these are

CONVERSATION ANALYSIS AND DISCURSIVE PSYCHOLOGY **15**

relevant to the interactions we are studying. This is in stark contrast to positioning theory and figured worlds discussed in Chapter 3 which largely focus on the role of power and status in interaction. So, in CA and DP in order to claim that any of these contextual features are relevant to the interaction they must show how the participants themselves orient to them in the interaction.

Another key principle of ethnomethodological approaches is that nothing in interaction can be decided *a priori* as irrelevant. Both what we say and how we say it are finely tuned to the interaction in which we are involved in and the recipients of our turns. Laughter, pauses, sniffs and hesitation markers such as *er* and *um* may all have interactional significance. This leads to the emphasis CA and DP research places on audio or video recordings and very detailed transcripts in their analysis.

One key difference between the research approaches discussed in this chapter and the other chapters is the role of the researcher in the process. The interest in this chapter is in how the participants themselves, teachers and students, are making sense of what is going on in the interaction and how they display this in the interaction, and not how the researcher makes sense of the interaction, for example by using existing theories to explain the structure of an interaction. The purpose of these approaches is to produce detailed descriptions of what is happening in an interaction, and how teachers and students are using the interaction to achieve particular things. It is also about making the 'common-sense' of classroom interaction explicit, which often means your findings will 'feel' familiar. This often means the analysis is of data that teachers and students themselves have collected.

Why do CA?

What is it that CA or DP offers us as researchers interested in classroom interaction? The micro analysis undertaken using CA or DP can take into consideration details and subtleties of interaction that are lost in other practices. It can explicate classroom practices that are often unconscious, unnoticed that also construct the interactional context of the classroom. This focus on detail enables us to say not only what people are doing, but also how they are doing it.

CA or DP studies are usually looking for recurring patterns or structures within the interactions. They are interested in how teachers and students do particular things, such as explaining or arguing, in their interactions. The structures within classroom interaction that have received the greatest amount of attention are those around turn-taking, preference and repair which now form tools that researchers can use to look at more classroom-specific structures, such as the structure of argumentation (e.g. Krummheuer (2007) explores the structures of argumentation in mathematics classrooms and Kim and Roth (2014) have explored the structures in science classrooms). These rules however are not meant in the mechanical or restraining sense. Instead they are more like norms where we can observe how participants orient to these rules, and deviation from them shows us both that these rules are usually oriented to, and also tell us a great deal as analysts about what people are doing in their turn design. In the sections that follow we outline the structures of turn-taking, preference organization and repair, as they relate to classrooms to give a sense of the analysis and tools CA researchers use when considering classroom interaction.

Turn-taking

Turn-taking has a very specific structure in classrooms that is different from everyday conversations or even other institutional contexts. Teachers generally control the opportunities to speak in their classrooms and have rights to speak that their students do not have. For example, if a teacher asks a question and a student gives an answer usually the next turn goes back to the teacher and not another student. This is commonly referred to as the IRE (Mehan 1979) or IRF (Sinclair and Coulthard 1975) pattern of interaction in discourse analysis and much of the literature (see Nind et al. 2016). The seminal work on classroom turn-taking using CA was done by Alex McHoul and is described in case example 2.1. This analysis was of 'formal talk' so does not cover all the types of talk that can occur in a classroom, but this structure remains dominant in many pedagogic interactions and forms the basis of subsequent analyses of turn-taking in classrooms, for example to show how in particular contexts the turn-taking differs from this structure, or to show how teachers can make use of this structure to achieve particular things (e.g. Ingram and Elliott 2016).

Case example 2.1:

The organization of turns at formal talk in the classroom (McHoul 1978)

Goal: The aim of the analysis was to describe in detail the structure of turn-taking that underlies teacher-led whole-class interactions. In particular, McHoul outlines how this structure differs from the previously identified structure of turn-taking in natural conversation (Sacks et al. 1974).

Outcomes: McHoul describes a set of rules for the taking of turns in classrooms. These rules involve different participation rights for teachers and students with teachers largely controlling who can speak when. First, when a teacher finishes speaking they then choose who speaks next or carry on speaking, no students other than the one selected can speak at this point. When a student finishes speaking it is the teacher who speaks next, and only if the teacher does not speak can the student continue to speak. If at this point both the teacher does not speak and the current student does not continue speaking, then other students may speak. In contrast to natural conversation these rules do not minimize the gap between speakers and more recent research has subsequently explored how this gap can affect how students participate in the classroom (Ingram and Elliott 2016; Rowe 1972).

Research methods: The data collected consisted of audio recordings of small group lessons in the UK and video recordings of lessons in Australia. The analysis involved detailed transcription and re-transcription, the listening to and re-listening to the video and audio recordings. McHoul uses both examples of these rules in action and examples of where the interaction deviates from these rules to show how the teacher and students orient to the rules in how they handle this deviation.

McHoul's detailed description allows us to focus in on interactions where this structure does not apply, such as a student speaking out of turn, and the consequences this has on the interaction, and potentially the teaching and learning. In Jenni's work (Ingram et al. 2018, 2019) on when students explain an idea, she found situations where a student gave an explanation in order to account for why they spoke out of turn. This explanation was not about the implicit structure of turn-taking but about the content of the lesson.

Preference organization

Within sequences of interaction some turns are 'preferred' over others. If you are asking a student a question, the preferred response would be an answer to your question for example. When analysing preference organization the focus is on how the first speaker enables the preferred response and how the second speaker responds to this by giving the preferred response or avoiding a dispreferred response. For example, a teacher's question is frequently pre-empted by references to knowledge and experiences that the students share and that the students can use to give the answer that the teacher is wanting, the preferred response. There are several possible responses that could be given to a teacher's question, but these responses are not equivalent, some are preferred over others.

This idea of preference refers to the structure of the sequence rather than any psychological idea (Schegloff 2007). Analysis looks at the structural features of the turns as well as the content to identify what the preferred responses and dispreferred responses are. Preferred turns are normally given immediately, whereas dispreferred turns often include hesitation and delay or some form of an account or explanation for why a dispreferred response is being given. The fact that dispreferred responses often include accounts gives rise to interactional contexts where students will give explanations, such as when they are disagreeing with a previously given answer, or when they are offering an answer without having the right to speak at that point.

A common teacher question in classrooms is 'do you understand' to which the preferred response is yes. This can be seen through the prevalence of yes being given to this response without any hesitation or demonstration that the students do understand. Teachers also do not always wait for a response to this question and move onto the next topic, treating the context as not needing further clarification or explanation. It is the yes response that is noticeably absent (Bilmes 1988) if the question is followed by no response. In contrast negative responses are given hesitantly or include an account of what is not understood.

Repair organization

Repair is both identification of and the treatment of any sort of trouble that arises when we interact. A repair is both initiated and performed, and these do not have to be done by the same person. For example, a student could indicate in some way that they have not understood what has just been said, but the teacher could perform the repair by rephrasing what has just been said. The 'trouble' may not be with the content of the interaction but could result from someone speaking when they are not expected to, or not speaking when they are expected to for example. Case example 2.2 describes a study that used the structure of repair to examine the differences between how teachers and teaching assistants interact with students.

Case example 2.2:

Opening up and closing down: How teachers and TAs manage turn-taking, topic and repair in mathematics lessons (Radford et al. 2011)

Context: The analysis presented in this particular paper was part of a larger study known as the DISS project (Deployment and Impact of Support Staff) which used a variety of methodologies to look at the relationship between the use of teaching assistants and other support staff and students' attainment and learning.

Goal: The purpose of this analysis was to use the tools of CA to give more detail and insight into the wider findings of the project. The project found that students who had teaching assistant support made less progress than those that did not, even after controlling for factors such as prior attainment and learning difficulties. The researchers also took advantage of the inductive nature of a CA approach to gain a 'fresh understanding of how the TA-student and teacher-student interactions compare whilst teaching the same lesson content' (p. 626).

Outcomes: The analysis of the interactions between the teacher and students and the teaching assistant and the students revealed differences in the structure and content of these interactions. In general, they found that teachers adopted inclusive teaching strategies that encouraged all their students to participate in whole-class interactions with a focus on learning by getting their students to reason, whereas teaching assistants focused specifically on task completion. They found that teachers opened up the talk with their students, while the teaching assistants closed it down. Finally, when students made mistakes teachers would usually offer prompts or hints to help their students self-correct these mistakes. In contrast the teaching assistants would usually supply the correct answer.

Research methods: The paper focused on three tools of CA in the analysis of the interactions: turn-taking, topic initiation and pursuit, and repair. The paper itself considers the interactions in four classrooms in the UK, two from year 5 (aged 9–10) and two from year 8 (aged 12–13) from four different schools, and compared the interactions between students and teachers and between students and teaching assistants.

Case example 2.2 illustrates how different participants in classrooms handle issues around repair differently, and in the case of the DISS study, teaching assistants performed repairs more often and in different ways to teachers. Research into the organization of repair in classrooms showed that teachers often initiate repairs but it is the students who perform the repair. In contrast, in ordinary conversation self-initiated self-repair is the preferred sequence (Liebscher and Dailey-O'Cain 2003; McHoul 1990). Furthermore, in ordinary conversation initiations of repair often begin with non-specific type of initiation and become more specific until the repair is performed, and teachers in general follow this structure when they initiate a repair, on the other hand students will usually use a specific type of repair initiation right from the start. One particular feature of classroom interaction is that teachers rarely explicitly assess a student's answer to a question as wrong. Teachers do a lot of interactional work to avoid saying 'no' and enabling students to self-correct when they make an error (Ingram et al. 2015).

Discursive psychology

DP is the study of how topics from psychology are used by people in interaction. These psychological topics and ideas are both topics within interaction and resources that we draw upon when we interact. DP makes use of the principles and tools of CA to examine topics usually studied by psychologists, such as knowing, understanding and beliefs. It makes no claims about what is going on inside participants' heads, instead DP focuses on how participants orient to doing cognition, such as remembering, within interactions. In this sense the focus is epistemological rather than ontological.

Case example 2.3:

Discursive psychology as an alternative perspective on mathematics teacher knowledge (Barwell 2013)

Goal: To show how DP can offer an alternative perspective on teacher knowledge through critiquing popular theories and categorizations used widely in educational research, specifically those based on Shulman's work (1986, 1987).

Outcomes: Two transcripts are analysed using first an approach based on categorizing teacher knowledge and then using DP. This analysis reveals the differences in approach, including the assumptions made about what teachers or students know and how the structure of teacher knowledge is conceptualized. Barwell exemplifies the difference in considering knowledge as something co-constructed in classroom interactions, from the perspective of the teacher and students in the interaction and the use of researchers' categorizations and frameworks.

Research methods: The paper uses two transcripts, one from a published article that categorizes teacher knowledge and takes a largely quantitative approach by coding video recordings. The transcript is offered in the original article as a case where a teacher has strong mathematical knowledge for teaching and high-quality mathematics instruction, as measured using the scales the authors had developed. These scales have their origins in Shulman's work. The second transcript comes from the author himself and from a study of multilingual primary classrooms in Canada.

Cognition is one topic considered both by DP and CA that is highly relevant to classroom-based research, where the focus is on teaching and learning. Conversational approaches to cognition treat topics in a very different way to the cognitive sciences and in the next section we focus on these differences.

Cognition

The relationships between cognition and language are complicated and disputed and we explore these further in Chapter 9. Both CA and DP take an epistemological approach to studying cognition where the focus is not what is going on in people's heads, for example what students are thinking, but how a shared understanding is constructed and maintained in interaction. This is consequently a valuable way of analysing how shared understandings are developed in classrooms. There is no attempt to, and no interest in, trying to understand what thinking, knowledge or understanding underlie what is being said. The focus of most classroom discourse-based research is teaching and learning, including what it means for students or teachers to know or understand something. CA and DP consider topics like understanding and knowing as interactional practices rather than cognitive states or processes. What is of interest is how students and teachers do knowing or treat each other as knowledgeable (or not).

One area in which there has been considerable research using CA and DP in classrooms is the treatment of knowledge and of people as knowledgeable. Epistemic management refers to how knowledge and understanding are treated in interaction and includes who has access to particular knowledge (epistemic access) (Heritage 2012a,b) and how teachers and students position themselves and each other in relation to this knowledge (epistemic stance), and in institutional settings such as classrooms epistemic rights and responsibilities (Stivers et al. 2011). In this approach, knowledge and understanding are not cognitive states, but rather interactional objects that participants negotiate and make observable.

For example, Koole (2012) looked at what happened in the interaction that followed a student stating that they did not understand while working on a task. The students in his corpus only indicated that they did not understand, not what they did not understand. This was sufficient for the teachers to give explanations but during these explanations there were no opportunities for the students to indicate if the explanation matched the problem they were having; these opportunities only arose at the end of the teacher's explanation. Thus, it is the teacher who has epistemic authority over the problem, not the student who has the problem.

Methods

Researchers using CA or DP work almost exclusively with audio and video recordings of interactions. Data needs to be naturally occurring so often these recordings are made without the researcher being present. In classrooms this often means teachers videoing themselves teaching by just leaving a camera on at the back of a classroom or leaving a digital voice recorder on students' desks. Naturally occurring interactions within studies of classroom interaction can also be taken to be those interactions that would have happened whether the researcher, or video or audio recorder was there or not. The distinction here is between naturally occurring data and naturally occurring activities. Video or audio recordings of classrooms can be collected specifically for research project, in which case they are produced as data, but they can also be collected for other reasons, such as for professional development activities within a school, in which case researchers need to turn this into data. These distinctions matter as both what was recorded and the way it in which it was recorded reflect the purposes of the original recording, which may not be the same as the researcher's purposes when they analyse these recordings. We will return to this issue in Chapter 12.

Process of analysis

For a lot of the time CA and DP researchers work with detailed transcripts of the audio or video data collected, usually using the Jefferson system of transcription (described in Chapter 13). This level of detail is required because of the premise that 'no order of detail in interaction can be dismissed a priori as disorderly, accidental, or irrelevant' (Heritage 1984: 241). Generally, the process begins through 'unmotivated looking', that is, without specific research questions or idea of what you are looking for. You might have an idea of where you might look for a phenomenon, for example the start of a lesson, instructions for group tasks etc. The process begins by noticing something or seeing something in the data and then building up a collection of cases. While each case is unique in that the context, participants and actions within an interaction are unique, by collecting cases that include a specific phenomenon CA allows you to identify features or structures that are context independent. As the collection builds it is possible to see commonalities in the cases as well as the boundaries of the phenomenon that is of interest. However, it is important to remember that it is the participants' orientation to the phenomenon that is of interest so cases need to include the sequence within which the phenomenon of interest occurs to enable us to analyse how the participants responded to the phenomenon. The *next-turn proof procedure* (Hutchby and Wooffitt 1998) refers to this idea in that it is the recipient's response that is where the evidence for any claim we want to make can be found as this shows how the recipient understood the phenomenon. Undertaking a CA involves oscillating between examining in detail particular cases and taking a synoptic view across the collection of cases built up.

Another important part of a CA is the consideration of deviant cases. These are cases where the recipient did not respond in the way you predicted from the analysis of the collection so far. These deviant cases usually give us the clearest evidence of the structures or norms around a particular phenomenon as often although the recipient has not given the expected response, they usually give an indication that they should have. For example, when not answering a question a recipient may apologize or offer an account or explanation for why they have not answered the question ('I don't know', for example). The question asker may also show in their subsequent turns that an answer was expected, for example by re-asking or re-formulating the question. The primacy of the participants' actions, interpretations or orientations also affects how CA researchers present their findings. Transcripts of interactions are always presented alongside the findings to allow the reader to draw conclusions from the data in the same way as the researcher has.

Conclusion

In this chapter we have given a brief introduction to the CA and DP approaches to research, focusing specifically on their application to classroom interaction. We have outlined some of the principles that underpin CA and DP research that mark them out as different from the other approaches discussed in this book and in other books in this series. It is these principles that guide research, rather than the usual set of methods or procedures that often drive what we do as researchers. These principles lead to what Seedhouse (2005) calls the 'CA mentality', a frame of mind which we bring to bear on our data.

These approaches are not without their challenges. You need to have the patience to work laboriously for hours on end at the production of detailed transcriptions that take into account all the details of the interaction, which in the case of classroom interaction is often very messy with lots of overlapping speech and sometimes many speakers at any point in time. Then the process of building collections of cases begins as you notice particular structures or phenomenon. The inductive approach often leads to interesting and useful findings, but not necessarily the ones you are intending to find when you begin the analysis. What these approaches do offer is fresh insight to how things are achieved in classroom interactions, how classes develop a shared understanding.

Further Reading

Edwards, D. and J. Potter (1992), *Discursive psychology*, London: Sage. This book introduces DP and explains its origins and theoretical underpinnings.

Sidnell, J. and T. Stivers (2012), *The handbook of conversation analysis*, Oxford: Wiley-Blackwell. This is a comprehensive guide to the structures and applications of CA and includes a chapter on DP and a chapter on the application of CA to classrooms.

Ten Have, P. (2007), *Doing conversation analysis* (2nd Edition), London: Sage. This is a nice introduction to CA, sufficient to get you started with CA research.

CHAPTER THREE

Positioning Theory and Figured Worlds

Introduction

This chapter is an introduction to positioning theory and figured worlds as theoretical approaches to analysing classroom discourse. Our introduction to these approaches will focus on the theoretical assumptions, methodologies and analytic tools, which are most relevant to education researchers. We begin with positioning theory and its position–action–storyline triad and modes of positioning, before outlining the connection to figured worlds. In the final section of this chapter we will explore the potential research areas and questions that positioning theory and figured worlds are most suited to address alongside examining the choices around methods available to researchers using these approaches.

Positioning theory has become a more prevalent approach to the analysis of classroom discourse over the last twenty years. Like CA and DP in the previous chapter, it takes a dynamic and flexible view of interaction and focuses on how people position themselves and each other, and are positioned by others in interaction, but goes beyond the types of interaction considered by CA and DP to include all forms of discourse and communication, such as the text in this book chapter for example. It has its roots in social psychology and was developed by Rom Harré and colleagues as a dynamic alternative to role theory. Positioning theory studies how people use language and communication for the 'accomplishment of various tasks and projects, jointly with others' (Harré and van Langenhove 1999: 3) and in particular the shifts and patterns of the rights and obligations of both speaking and acting as we interact with others.

The premise is that positioning takes place 'whenever and wherever people get together and do or say things that make sense only in the uptake of other (and sometimes that other may be "myself" in another guise)' (Harré and van Langenhove 1999: 199). The idea of positioning is widely used in a range of theories and disciplines, but what Harré and colleagues did was narrow the focus to the actual moments of interaction while still taking into account the broader cultural and social contexts in which the interaction occurs. It is the bringing together of these two levels of interest that draws many researchers to positioning theory (and figured worlds). Analysis focuses on both how positions shift in interactions and how they are constituted in the interactions. This contrasts with role theory where roles people have or take are relatively static. When we interact with other people how we make sense of what is being said is shaped by our understanding of the positions of the other people in the interaction. Whenever we interact we position ourselves in particular ways, but simultaneously we also position others.

Positioning theory shares many of the same assumptions and premises as DP described in the previous chapter, as both are discursive approaches within social psychology. Both positioning theory and DP treat attitudes, positions and identities as constituted in interaction in local contexts rather than as something belonging to the individual. Similarly, they treat these psychological notions, and classroom practices, as being both maintained and transformed through the interactions that occur in the classroom. Positioning theory, however, is broader in its focus, drawing upon wider social and cultural influences on discourse and the use of storylines described in the next section marks out this difference in particular.

We begin this chapter by outlining some of the key constructs of positioning theory, including speech acts, positions and storylines as they apply to classrooms. Our purpose in this chapter is to examine the analytic tools that positioning theory and related frameworks offer for analysing classroom discourse in its broadest sense. We include a discussion of figured worlds which shares many similarities with positioning theory but with more of a focus on identities and agency, and clear roots in anthropology rather than the social psychology associated with positioning theory research.

The position–action–storyline triad

Any analysis using positioning theory draws upon three key constructs: speech acts; positions or positionings; and storylines. Slocum and van Langenhove (2004: 233) describe a 'mutually determining triad' illustrating the relationship between these three constructs that models the interactions between the social positions taken by those in the interaction, the particular acts used that objectify these social positions, and the discursive context that makes particular storylines relevant. Various versions of this triad appear in the positioning theory literature, some labelling the vertices and others the edges, some replacing social forces with speech act (e.g. Harré et al. 2009). These three constructs operate at different levels of analysis which allows us to take into account the in-the-moment interactions alongside the broader social and cultural contexts (storylines) that might be influencing the interaction.

Positioning consists of positions and storylines that influence and constrain the possible actions and meanings of speech acts. Speech actions are the words or actions that teachers and students use when interacting and speech acts are the meanings that they ascribe to these words or actions. The analysis of speech acts is similar to the way utterances are analysed in CA (Chapter 2).

A position is described by Harré and van Langenhove as a 'metaphorical concept through reference to which a person's "moral" and personal attributes as a speaker are compendiously collected' (1999: 17) which are 'structured in various ways, which impinges on the possibilities of interpersonal, intergroup and even intrapersonal action through some assignment of such rights, duties and obligations to an individual as are sustained by the cluster' (1999: 1). Positions describe the types of rights, obligations and duties that teachers and students draw on as they interact and the analysis of discourse focuses on how these rights, obligations and duties are constructed, maintained or contested. Rights are seen as what others in the interaction must do for you while duties are what you must do for them (Moghaddam et al. 2008).

Storylines are broader concepts that include shared repertoires or narratives that influence what is expected in an interaction and include conventions or norms. In particular, storylines describe what the participants understand to be the sort of situation they are interacting in (Slocum and van Langenhove 2004: 233). Storylines can also be implicit or explicit. Explicit ones are where positions are pre-decided and particular participants take particular positions because of the context in which the interaction is taking place, such as the positions of teacher and student. However, from a research perspective, it can be difficult to identify the relevant storylines as there can be several influencing the interaction at any time, and each participant's perspective about which storylines are relevant might be different. Storylines can also be embedded within other storylines and include positions and relationships between participants.

Researchers using positioning theory usually focus on positions and how storylines and speech acts affect positions and positioning. These positions within the classroom are observable, as teachers and students bring with them different rights, obligations and duties when they interact. Some of these rights and obligations come from their institutional roles as teacher or student and some are negotiated in the interaction itself. A position refers to the clustering of these rights, obligations and duties, but importantly, not everyone in an interaction has equal access to rights and duties to perform particular actions (Harré 2012: 196). For example, teachers and students have different rights over the types of comments they can make in classrooms but also the same comments (speech act) can have a different meaning depending on whether it is said by a student or a teacher. During interactions teachers and students can also ascribe rights, claim rights or place duties on each other. These positions are ephemeral, and it is the shifts and changes in positions and positioning that is usually the focus of analysis. Figured worlds, discussed below, takes a very similar approach to positioning theory but the analysis usually focuses on storylines and positioning within these storylines.

Positioning theory departs from other theories that make use of speech acts in that meaning is not drawn from the intentions of the speakers but instead from how words and actions are used in interaction. One utterance can be multiple speech acts (Davies and Harré 1999: 34), it can perform several different functions at the same time, which is what makes them available for negotiation.

Different positions and storylines can affect and constrain the speech acts associated with some utterances. Some authors now use the phrase communication acts to make it clear that gestures, body position etc. are also involved in positioning, but Harré and colleagues use the phrase speech acts inclusively to include gestures, actions and pauses. This is the same as the approach taken by CA and DP except that with positioning theory these speech acts can be considered in isolation from the surrounding speech acts, or the sequence of interaction, as it is the broader interactional context that is of interest.

The distinction between positions and storylines can be a difficult one to make when analysing data. Take, for example, gender; some researchers treat gender as a positioning while others treat it as a storyline. The reciprocal relationship between positions and storylines contributes to the complexity of teasing out the difference. In practice, gender is both positioning and a storyline and the way you treat it depends on the aim and focus of your analysis.

Modes of positioning

Harré and colleagues make several analytic distinctions between different modes of positioning which have evolved over time as the theory has developed and can be used as tools by researchers to analyse classroom discourse. In each speech act there will be many modes of positioning involved. These modes include moral, personal, self or reflexive, other or interactive, tacit or unintentional, intentional, deliberate or performative, forced or accountive, strategic, first-order, second-order and third-order positioning. In this chapter we will briefly describe each of these modes as part of a positioning theory analytic framework but most researchers will focus on only two or three contrasting modes; for example, Yoon in case example 3.1 uses intentional self-positioning and interactive positioning in her analysis. Moral and personal positioning are separated by whether the positioning refers to a particular position, such as teacher, in which case it is a moral positioning, or the personal attributes of the person doing the positioning or being positioned in which case it is personal positioning. Generally, positioning acts involve aspects of both moral and personal positioning.

Self-positioning or reflexive position refers to how we position ourselves. We might do this by referring to events in our past, making requests or giving instructions, or giving explanations or instructions, for example. Deliberate self-positioning is often marked by the use of the pronoun I in speech acts. Forced self-positioning occurs when it is someone else who initiates the need for your self-positioning, for example by asking 'how are you?' which requires you to talk about yourself. In the classroom, forced self-positioning occurs when a teacher asks a student to account for their behaviour in some way. Other or interactive positioning is where we position someone else in interaction, so that they act in particular ways. These can be both intentional and unintentional and can be accepted or contested. It is also important to remember that the positioning of self and other are mutually determining as when we position ourselves we are also positioning the others in the interaction and vice versa. By positioning yourself as a teacher, you are also positioning the others in the interaction as students. These positions then become resources that those within the interaction can draw upon as the interaction continues.

Case example 3.1:

Uninvited guests: The influence of teachers' roles and pedagogies on the positioning of English language learners in the regular classroom (Yoon 2008)

Context: This was a study of regular classroom teachers who had English language learners (ELLs) in their classrooms. All the teachers were middle school English language arts teachers who had not received any professional development on how to teach students who were ELLs.

Goal: To examine the relationship between teachers' views about their roles as a teacher, as an English language arts teacher and as a teacher of students who are ELLs and their practice in the classroom.

Outcomes: The analysis identified three different ways in which the teachers positioned themselves, as a teacher for all students, as a teacher for regular education students or as a teacher for their particular subject. These positions also included different roles for the ELLs as having diverse needs or linguistic needs. These different positions were connected to the way the ELLs participated in lessons and contrasted those that were positioned as powerful, strong students and those positioned as powerless, poor students. Only the teacher who positioned themselves as a teacher for all students invited the ELLs to participate in the lesson actively.

Research methods: This study used a 'collective case study' method (Stake 1995). One class from each of the teachers was observed most days for a term, focusing specifically on two students who were ELLs. The same students were then also observed in their English as a Second Language (ESL) lessons later the same day. The teachers and the focus students were also interviewed several times. For two of the teachers involved, the ELL students were the only ELL students in the classroom. For the third teacher, the ELL students were chosen specifically because their participation in their regular lessons was different from their participation in their ESL lessons. The analysis specifically focused on how the teachers offered or limited opportunities for the students to participate, but also on how other students in the classroom affected these opportunities. Two modes of positioning from Harré's work were drawn upon in the analysis: intentional self-positioning and interactive positioning.

In this case example, Yoon shows how the different ways that teachers self-positioned affected how ELLs were positioned in classroom interactions. In particular, these self-positionings affected the participation of different learners during classwork. This case example illustrates how positioning theory can be used to look at the relationship between beliefs and practice, as self-positioning takes into account peoples' stated beliefs and practice is observable through the speech acts. It also illustrates how the teachers' self-positioning affects students' self-positioning.

First-order positioning describes how people locate themselves and others and is usually implicit. For example, if a teacher says to a student 'sit down' the teacher is positioning themselves as someone who has the authority to make such a demand, but also positions the student as someone who should follow this teacher's demands. However, if these positions are challenged or are negotiated then this becomes second-order positioning and it is this challenge or negotiation that makes the positioning explicit. If the student sits down following the teacher's request, then there is no challenge to the positioning done in the speech act 'sit down' and the storyline will continue uninterrupted. However, if the student challenges this request in some way, such as by refusing to sit down, then the positioning of the teacher as someone with the authority to make such a request, and/or the positioning of the student as someone who needs to follow the teacher's requests is questioned. The teacher will then need to justify these positions in some way. There is also third-order positioning which occurs outside of the original interaction as people talk (or write) about or re-tell the interaction or story. Both second-order and third-order positionings must be intentional, whereas first-order positioning can be either intentional or unintentional.

Davies and Harré (1990) argue that all individuals view the world from a certain position, and this self-positioning or reflexive positioning influences their actions in a given context. So, for example, teachers could position themselves as teachers of a particular subject, or they could position themselves as teachers of children. This self-positioning will affect how these teachers interact with their students in their classrooms. On the other hand, interactive positioning involves one person positioning another. This positioning can offer opportunities or limit what the other participants can do or say. In classroom studies this positioning often includes positioning someone as competent or incompetent (or deficient in some way); this may be particularly the case where we are studying the ways in which different groups of students are positioned in contrast to others (as in case example 3.1).

In case example 3.2, the analysis focuses more on the role of storylines in the learning of science. In this project, positioning theory is just one of many theoretical approaches used to analyse the classroom data and accompanying interviews but is used here to illustrate the negotiation between one student's personal storyline and the official storyline of the science classroom.

Case example 3.2:

Science students' classroom discourse: Tasha's Umwelt (Arnold 2012)

Context: The case presented in this paper comes from a large research programme based at the University of Melbourne that focused on a range of classroom practices, in a range of curriculum areas, and drawing on a range of different theoretical frameworks. Arnold's analysis sits within this, was the focus of her doctoral work and is a study of the classroom interactions from a sequence of secondary science lessons filmed in a specifically designed research classroom.

Goal: To develop an understanding of the way students make meaning in secondary school science. The analysis focused on addressing the questions: How can discursive practices employed by students in their science classroom be described? How do students use psychological categories in their talk in and about their science classroom? How are students positioned, and how do they position themselves within science classroom discourses?

Outcomes: The presentation of the episodes of small group interactions showed how at times Tasha positioned herself as an outsider to the culture of science and at other times as a competent participant. Arnold argues that these positionings are part of locally negotiated practices rather than attributes of Tasha herself. The practices observed in the science classroom are not predetermined by the context of it being a science classroom but are co-constructed by the students as they negotiate what it means to do science in that particular classroom. In particular, the relationship between the storyline of 'official discourses' and the personal storyline (or umwelt) of Tasha illustrates how storylines interact, are negotiated, and contested in interaction.

Research methods: Nine consecutive science lessons were video- and audio-recorded. The use of a research classroom meant that this involved four video cameras and seven audio tracks. In addition, two groups of students and the teacher participated in post-lesson interviews and included Tasha. These interviews were conducted on an individual basis and participants were asked to play sections of the lesson video that were personally important to them. Additionally, written materials including the students' work were collected.

The analysis focused specifically on student talk about themselves during the lessons and in particular, where the students used personal pronouns or emotive or epistemic verbs and identified the ways in which the students used and constructed categories of X. The article reports on the positions and positioning of one particular student, Tasha, who often positioned herself as less knowledgeable than her peers. The focus is on the personal history of Tasha as she conceives it and how she draws upon this personal history as she interacts in the science classroom.

Figured Worlds

The concept of figured worlds developed at the same time as positioning theory and draws upon many of the same ideas, but with a specific focus on (positional) identity and agency. It was first introduced by Holland et al. (1998) in their seminal book *Identity and Agency in Cultural Worlds* and has its roots in anthropology and cultural studies while drawing upon key ideas from social psychology. Figured worlds are defined as 'socially and culturally constructed realm[s] of interpretation in which particular characters and actors are recognised, significance is assigned to certain acts, and particular outcomes are valued over others' (1998: 52). The concept of figured worlds emphasizes the storylines and cultural narratives within which we interact. While actions, activities and practices are all part of how figured worlds are constructed and maintained, the durable storylines are of primary interest.

Holland et al. (1998) specifically developed the concept of positional identity, characterizing patterns of participation (in the sense of Wenger) in which people comply with or resist prevalent ways of participation in figured worlds. Figured worlds are a model of identity that emphasizes the ways that people perform and narrate stories about both themselves and others. Similar to both positioning theory and DP, it is the context in which we are participating in that determines the types of identities that are available. Again, figured worlds are dynamic. We can make use of particular storylines as we interact, but this use of storylines also reshapes the figured worlds we are acting within.

Research drawing upon the concept of figured worlds usually draws heavily on interview data alongside the analysis of classroom interactions in order to identify the storylines and figured worlds of both teachers and students. The figured world of the classroom may include storylines of memorization and developing particular skills, or it may include storylines of making connections and reasoning for example. These storylines not only have implications for the identities that the students negotiate as they act within the figured world of a particular classroom, but also the ways in which teachers position these students. A currently topical storyline in education around the world is often referred to as 'the achievement gap'. This storyline involves considering different educational outcomes for particular groups of students, such as those of a particular race, social class and gender. Thus, the underachievement of a particular student is often explained by recruiting this storyline and drawing on the student's characteristics that would make the storyline of the achievement gap relevant. We return to figured worlds in Chapter 7 to illustrate its use in identity research.

Why choose positioning theory?

Positioning theory's strength is in that it examines interaction at different levels. It takes into account both the actions within an interaction and the broader social and cultural influences on these actions. Positioning theory is most useful when looking at issues around power, hegemony and authority in classroom interaction, whether that is between a teacher and their students, or within groups of students, as it was in case example 3.1. It is also used to examine how different practices are experienced differently by different students, and how storylines either persist or change as positionings are negotiated and contested, as illustrated in case example 3.2.

Positioning theory is ideal for situations where you want to combine an analysis of the co-construction of particular positions in interaction while also considering the context within which this interaction occurs, where this context includes the personal histories of interactions as well as established societal roles. It is most useful when you want to capture multiple stories that arise in interaction, treating these stories as contextualized within the school or classroom environment in which they occur. As an approach, it acknowledges the complexity of classroom discourse while offering the analytic tools to focus on specific parts of this complexity. As it draws on a wider range of discourse than the previously discussed methods, it enables us to look at how classroom interactions are influenced by particular artefacts or tools, including textbooks and technology, as Anderson did in case example 3.3.

Case example 3.3:

Applying positioning theory to the analysis of classroom interactions: Mediating micro-identities, macro-kinds and ideologies of knowing (Anderson 2009)

Context: This paper examined data collected as part of a longer three-year project in the United States where the researchers were attempting to change the practice of mathematics teaching in one school to encourage students to talk more about mathematics and work collaboratively in mathematics lessons. The school had been identified as being 'at risk' because of low achievement scores. The researchers introduced an intervention that involved students working on problems individually for twenty minutes, before sharing their reasoning in groups of four and then coming to a shared understanding of each of the problems as a group. Following this group work, the students had to evaluate the discussions using a 'conversation rubric' designed by the researchers.

Goal: To use positioning theory to address three research questions: How is participation recognized across a set of classroom activities? How are forms of participation differentially valued? What opportunities to learn are afforded students as a result of negotiating contexts for participation across activities?

Outcomes: Anderson develops the analytic framework within positioning theory to include mediating factors, such as learning goals, resources such as textbooks as well as interactions between students, and between the teacher and students. This results in four levels of mediation, enabling her to example interactions, positioning and ideologies at the micro, meso and macro levels.

She also uses the construct of *kinds* of people (figured subjects) to describe ways of interacting that link their communicative acts to particular labels or characterizations over time. The analysis shows how individual students are positioned as a particular kind of person over time, even when their behaviour changes during this time and contradicts the positioning of others.

Research methods: The small group classroom interactions from one classroom in the United States with students aged ten to eleven years were video-recorded, and their written work was collected. The data was collected from five mathematics lessons that formed the intervention over a period of fourteen weeks and the analysis focuses on the interactions of just one small group with four students in it.

In case example 3.3, positioning theory is supplemented with an additional analytic framework, enabling a focus on the mediating role of different interactions or artefacts. Other researchers have also taken this approach of combining positioning theory with other frameworks to structure the analysis. For example, Herbel-Eisenmann et al. (2015) use Lemke's (2000) idea of timescales to address the complexity of working at different scales, particularly in relation to storylines that can be embedded within other storylines and can operate at different scales.

As well as topics around power and authority, issues that are specific to the classroom where positioning theory may be particularly fruitful include positions associated with expertise and competence. This is particularly interesting when considering peer-to-peer interaction where the positions of expert and novice often take more interactive work to construct and negotiate as they are not usually predetermined through pre-established roles. The role of teacher usually carries with it the position of expert, and hence in interactions, the teacher's knowledge is usually accepted and rarely challenged. Where expertise and competence are negotiated, as is usually the case in group work, positionings and speech acts will include reasons, justifications and demonstrations of expertise available to the researcher, which may also give us insight into the relationship between positioning and learning. This may also suggest the importance of group work where students need to give reasons and appeal to warrants in order to demonstrate expertise.

Methods

While all studies using positioning theory use audio or video recordings of interactions, these are often supplemented with interviews. Interviews enable us to look at the different interpretations the different students have of the same speech acts or the same interactions. This could lead to contrasting the experiences of students labelled as privileged according to a particular storyline and those labelled as underprivileged. Interviews can also be used to ask about participants' beliefs and attitudes, which gives us insight into how they self-position themselves. Studies using positioning theory often include interview data alongside classroom data in order to gain access to the historical contexts that the participants see as relevant to the interaction, as in case example 3.2. It is important to be careful that you are collecting the storylines of your participants, and not imposing your own storylines as a researcher! In contrast to the CA and DP approach to data analysis, there are no specific strategies or conventions as to how the data is analysed. Some researchers divide the data into episodes, defined as 'any sequence of happenings in which human beings engage which has some principle of unity' (Harré and van Langenhove 1999: 4). This is a very flexible definition that has been used by researchers in a variety of ways. Others focus on an individual student or teacher and identify all the self-positioning acts performed by them, or alternatively all the positionings that involve them, including where they are positioned by others. Some researchers use narratological analysis to uncover the implicit storylines and then identify positionings relevant to these storylines in the interaction.

A common technique is to examine the use of pronouns in interaction to look at the extent to which speakers take responsibility for what they are saying. The use of the first person pronoun, I, as well as indicating some form of self-positioning, indicates that the speaker has personal responsibility for what they are saying. In contrast, the use of 'me', while still a first person pronoun, is reflexive and indicates that the speaker sees themselves from the perspective of others. The use of 'we' as a collective pronoun can indicate a shared sense of responsibility with other members of a particular group, but also can position the utterance as more authoritative. In contrast, the use of 'you' deflects responsibility to the other individual or individuals in the interaction, but also can be used to reference the category of student in general. Each of these pronouns is used in a variety of ways, particularly by teachers, and the speech acts including these pronouns are affected by this choice of pronoun.

One of the biggest challenges facing researchers using positioning theory is how the local interactions and the storylines, or cultural narratives, actually inform each other. Harré and colleagues treat positions and storylines as simultaneously emergent in the moment, but then this raises the question of how you distinguish between the process and the category (e.g. doing expertise and being an expert). This challenge has been approached in many different ways, including through the concept of figured worlds, but remains a tension that needs careful consideration.

Conclusion

This chapter introduced positioning theory as a potential theoretical and analytical framework for researching classroom discourse. There is a great deal of flexibility in how you might use positioning theory, as illustrated by the three case examples, and in contrast to CA research described in Chapter 2. Consequently, there are also many reasons as to why positioning theory might be used to address a wide range of research questions and issues. However, at the heart of most research using this approach are issues around power, difference and privilege.

Further Reading

Harre, R. and L. van Langenhove (1999), *Positioning theory: Moral contexts of intentional action*, Oxford: Blackwell. This book introduces positioning theory and is useful to gain a sense of how it has been applied in research outside of education, but using concepts and ideas that are relevant to classroom-based research.

Herbel-Eisenmann, B. A. A., D. Wagner, K. R. R. Johnson, H. Suh and H. Figueras (2015), 'Positioning in mathematics education: Revelations on an imported theory', *Educational Studies in Mathematics*, 89 (2): 185–204. https://doi.org/10.1007/s10649-014-9588-5. This paper is useful for its critique of positioning theory both in its conceptualization and in the ways that some researchers within mathematics education have used it.

CHAPTER FOUR

Critical Discourse Analysis

Introduction

'Discourse analysis' is somewhat of an umbrella term that is used by different people to convey different things. This chapter explores a particular approach to discourse analysis and where it sits under that umbrella term. We define what 'a discourse' is, consider what makes CDA 'critical', and look at a step by step guide in how to carry out CDA. The difficulty is in what the word 'discourse' conveys, a problem which we raised in the introduction. There we defined discourse in the way we use it in the title of this book as 'any spoken or written expression of meaning, interaction, or other forms of interaction such as gesture or eye gaze, or the way people dress'. Discourse analysis can be an analysis which has discourse as its data source, the material on which it works. But it can also (and more technically correctly) be an analysis which finds what discourses are present in the data. The next section defines 'a discourse' as we mean it in this way.

Many analyses which are called discourse analysis are simply thematic or content analyses – ones which find the main themes in a data set or measure the presence and dominance of certain content. (For a longer explanation of content analysis see Chapter 10 'Written Texts'.) For these kinds of research, which we do not cover in this book, you may want to consult a text on qualitative data analysis, a suggestion for which is given in further reading (Saldana 2015).

What is a discourse?

'A discourse' in language is 'a system of statements which cohere around common meanings and values' (Hollway 1983: 131). For example, 'No Child Left Behind' became a strong discourse in the US education system in the early twenty-first century. This discourse is named after the Act which introduced a variety of measures and an ambition to close the attainment gap between students in US schools. But the discourse itself was a much wider and more influential one; it then developed to encompass the high-stakes testing measures which ensued, and the discourse subtly shifted to include the washback effects these policies had had. A discourse within a school might be related to its school motto: Victoria's local school motto is 'Success for Everyone', which in itself demonstrates how dominant this discourse has become across different contexts. Another local school has 'Be the Best You Can Be'. Although these mottoes are not discourses on their own, if their influence is present and reflected in the language used by the teachers, students, governors and parents in spoken or written communication, they become discourses. There are still more ways in which we might use the word 'discourse' (media discourse, gendered discourse, racist discourse (see Wodak 2014)); this makes it crucial that discourse analysts define their use of the term carefully and that we make sure when reading discourse analysis (and especially CDA) that we understand the way in which this piece of research is using the term.

What is 'critical' about CDA?

CDA brings together linguistic (discourse) analysis with social and cultural theory in order to use linguistic means to answer questions about society. The word 'critical' in education research often refers to considering the way in which power is distributed and implemented, whether it is official power or societal power. CDA draws on the work of theorist Michel Foucault, who argues that power is constituted through discourse and is implicated in what is constructed as knowledge (Foucault 1990).

Power is found within language in the ways that it acts to constitute social realities. It is important to remember, however, that this is not necessarily power used for the worst. As Rogers and colleagues remind us, power 'can take on both liberating and oppressive forms' (2005: 369).

One of the jobs of CDA is to challenge beliefs and discourses which are hegemonic – the current status quo – by amplifying challenges to those discourses and examining how they are themselves constructed and constructing (Gunter et al. 2014). CDA enables the researcher to explore contradictions, tensions and power structures which exist within education's systems and policies (Rogers et al. 2005). It is therefore particularly widely used in relation to education policy. These policies are still 'classroom discourse' in that they influence what happens in classrooms and can in turn affect and be affected by what teachers and pupils say and do in classrooms. For example, national discourses about educational achievement and examinations can have a powerful presence in the classrooms of those who are about to undertake those examinations. 'Critical' does not mean 'negative', it is important to note, as it might in everyday usage, but refers to an intellectual challenge and engagement with the source material and topic. Having said that, most CDA is used as a form of challenge to social or political practices which the researchers dislike (Wodak 2014).

Foucauldian CDA is a form of CDA which considers the ways in which language is used to construct people in particular ways, specifically in what they have agency in and what they do not have agency in. It pays particular effect to social structures and the effect of discourses upon social realities. An example would be the 'undeserving versus deserving poor' discourse which has formed part of political language in Britain since the nineteenth century (Dorling 2010).

Critical theory as a whole is concerned with a whole raft of injustices; critical race theory, postcolonial theory and queer theory are just a few examples. The common belief that critical theorists share is that 'facts are never neutral and are always embedded in contexts' (Rogers et al. 2005: 368). CDA is usually focused on a particular social problem, and moves backwards and forwards between theory and data to illuminate that problem.

Case example 4.1 shows a study with a deliberate critical aim that specifically sought to illuminate an educational policy and how it had been enacted.

Case example 4.1:

A critical discourse analysis of the new labour discourse of social and emotional learning (SEL) across schools in england and wales: conversations with policymakers (Emery 2016)

Context: A study of the policy promoting SEL in schools under the New Labour government in England and Wales (1997–2010), concerned with children's ability to understand, express and manage their emotions.

Goal: To conduct a CDA of the New Labour (1997–2010) discourse of SEL in schools, and how it was understood and enacted by policymakers, via a set of interviews with high-level policy actors.

Outcomes: SEL policy took different shapes in England and Wales but in both countries was founded on certain discursive practices. The article used interdiscursivity (which Emery glosses as 'a series of connected powerful whispers' [2016: 17]) as an example to illustrate the discourses of 'neoliberal, self-managing, entrepreneur in England, and social democratic, collaborative, citizen in Wales' (Emery 2016: 21). These discourses were produced and distributed through written texts such as school programmes for SEL and through talk reported in the media. In Wales this was part of a larger contemporaneous nation-building narrative in the wake of devolution.

Methods: The researcher conducted two-hour interviews with each of eight elite participants who had been centrally involved in SEL policy and implementation, four each from England and Wales, representing a government minister, head of a relevant Civil Service Department (Children, Health, Education), a senior government advisor and a head of an SEL campaign group. These interviews were then coded according to 'discursive practice (the production, distribution and consumption of SEL); text (grammar, use of nouns, genres and discourse orders used by the interviewees) and the social practice (broader social/cultural/economic/political events)' (Emery 2016: 16). Any given utterance might be in more than one of these categories; these coded data chunks were then considered in relation to the researchers' research questions.

Language as social practice

Throughout this book we have considered language as part of a network of social practices. Language is both affected by the context in which it is used and also affects that context. For example, think about the use of the word 'mate' to refer to a pupil by a teacher. Now what if the pupil used the word 'mate' to refer to the teacher? This would only be possible in certain social contexts, but it could also affect the way the entire class related to the teacher in future. Discourses constitute social realities; they are affected by them and they also create them.

On a larger scale, think of the ways in which teen mothers are constructed by the way that the media and politicians talk about them. In the 1980s and 1990s in Britain the most common discourse about teen mothers was of the 'council flat'; the allegation that teens deliberately fell pregnant in order to leapfrog the queue for social housing. A counter narrative is of the 'exceptional mother' who gives birth and immediately goes back to study for, and pass, her school leaving exams. The construction of those young women as extraordinary actually reinforces the underlying discourse that teen mothers are dropouts and failures. CDA is a way in which we can investigate how social realities are constructed by and with language.

Doing CDA

There is a 'customary disclaimer' (Arribas-Ayllon and Walkerdine 2008: 91) in CDA research papers that there is no set way in which to carry out CDA research. It is considered to be an approach rather than a method, in that it is constituted by the attitudes and aims rather than by the specific steps which are carried out by the researcher. As Hore (2014) has pointed out, this reticence is rather an imitation of Foucault, who might be described as father of this approach, who said 'I take care not to dictate how things should be' (Foucault 1994: 288). However, since this is not very helpful to the novice researcher, we will outline here one way of doing CDA. In the case examples in this chapter are four different approaches and reading the articles they come from shows vastly differing ways of writing about how they conceive of CDA, and how they did it. Emery, the author of case example 4.1, suggests that one of the reasons that there is relatively little CDA research published in journals is the difficulty of making it 'thin sliced' (2016: 21) to fit in with word limits, because of the need to explain precisely the theoretical and methodological frameworks underlying any given study.

The underlying assumption of CDA is that social reality is constituted by language and that language has the power to do things to people, by the way it positions them in the minds of others, and in the way it leads them into particular paths of belief. Case example 4.2 relates a study of a group of teachers looking at narratives of immigrants in young adult literature, and the effect that this had both upon their understanding of immigrants, but also their constructions of themselves as socially just and aware adults.

Case example 4.2:

Teachers' discourses about immigrants and their experiences within the realm of children's and young adult literature (Graff 2010)

Context: A study of K-12 and collegiate US educators enrolled in a graduate course on the construction of immigrants in multicultural literature.

Goal: To examine the ways in which the educators constructed themselves and immigrants during and after the course.

Outcomes: Immersion in and discussion of literature involving immigrants cultivated educators' awareness of hegemonic policies and practices towards immigrants in the United States. The study shows a movement of teachers' understanding of immigrants as initially a 'thing' that was distant from them and their concerns, through a period where they constructed themselves as more socially aware and more informed teachers and citizens, who conceived of community as heterogeneous rather than homogeneous. They engaged with discourses which were prominent in media treatment of immigrants, such as 'Assimilation', and negotiated their understanding of how these discourses fit into their own newly constructed identities. Graff positions these outcomes as a testament to the power of story to enable effective transformation of understanding and ideas; she also sees her participants as 'trying on' new linguistic identities and practices (such as reading choices) that fit with their new identities as those with more understanding of the immigrant experience and more desire for social justice.

Methods: The study involved twelve of the nineteen students on a course on written and pictorial narratives of immigrants in children's literature, supported by the use of empirical data taken from sociological or political research. They were all practising educators enrolled in graduate study. The data which was collected included 'personal response journals', outcomes of class activities, the researcher's notes about the seminar (she was also the course lead) and one interview with each teacher, conducted a year after the course, to elicit the ongoing impact. The data was then analysed in a multi-layered process which began with a thematic analysis derived from the data and the literature, and moved on to a CDA to consider the reciprocal ways in which the teachers created their own identities through the course, and crafted identities for immigrants.

Case example 4.3 similarly shows how exposure to particular types of language about ecology and humans can affect the way in which students grow up to understand the environmental challenges facing the world today as related to human agency.

Case example 4.3:

Human–nature relationships in school science (Sharma and Buxton 2015)

Context: The role of science education in preparing students to understand the complex environmental challenges facing the world.

Goal: To examine the textual representations of the relationships between human societies and natural environmental systems in a popular seventh-grade textbook in Georgia in the United States.

Outcomes: The language of science textbooks has major implications for students' 'ecological literacy' (2015: 60). The textbook in the study demonstrated outdated representations of the interrelatedness of human society and natural systems. The language of the textbook suppressed the concept of human agency in relation to material changes in the environment, often through the use of the passive voice. Where agency is recorded it is often as the generic 'people' rather than as the result of 'globalized exploitation of land and natural resources by corporations' (2015: 272). Similarly the effect of environmental threats such as pollution is minimized by their representation, particularly on marginalized communities. Climate change was not mentioned as an 'environmental challenge' at all. This textbook is chosen by a State Advisory Committee, that is, by a sociopolitical body; the authors conclude that the language in the book works to reinforce a certain sociopolitical view of ecology.

Methods: The study used a CDA of the language in a textbook which is used in the year in which students in Georgia are introduced to fundamental concepts of ecology. The analysis utilized several rounds of close reading of each chapter, culminating in a content-level analysis that addressed the question of the characterization of the relationship between humans and the environment. This was supplemented by a clause-level micro analysis of the linguistic structures used, to understand *how* these characterizations were achieved. The authors used Hallidayan functional linguistics as a framework for this micro analysis, looking at processes and actors that were represented within each clause.

A first step is to establish the data set which you are using and its limits. Discourses are widespread and complex, moving between talk and written documents; discourses set on the national stage by politicians and the media find expression on the local level, in classrooms and home. Any data set can be appropriate for CDA; the case examples show the use of a single textbook, a varied set of classroom talk data, a set of interviews and a set of data comprising written reflective journals, classroom exercises and interviews with participants. It is always a good idea to have a justification for 'why this data set?', and for the reasons behind inclusion or exclusion criteria, whether or not they are formally laid out.

When the data set has been established, read through the texts several times. CDA is a qualitative methodology which depends on the interpretative power of the researcher. This has implications because the identity of the researcher has the power to strongly affect the research outcomes, a point which is considered in the next section on 'positionality'. Research questions help to guide the things which a researcher notices as they read through the text. Case example 4.3 used their research questions to guide them to notice content which represented relationships between human and natural systems. A Foucauldian might look for particular discursive objects: so, for example, in a study looking at feedback and assessment, we might consider the things that feedback is constructed as being able to do. That is, it might be constructed as being able to make students feel more positive, as being able to improve outcomes, as being able to show that teachers are acting professionally and as being able to demonstrate the school's commitment to the use of educational research evidence. These discursive objects may be the main outcome of the analysis of the text, or they may all relate to one thing, such as in case example 4.2 where the ways in which the teachers constructed themselves as socially concerned and informed citizens was the main focus of the discursive constructions through the data, as it developed over time. If you have more than one researcher on the project, it is helpful to have them read through the text independently and see what they each notice.

However, there is a further stage. When a read through has collected the different discursive objects or noticeable items in the text, these can be collated into a list, and different ways of grouping them considered. These groups are the named discourses within the data set: and therefore the name which is given to them is important and also highly dependent on the researcher. Discourses in this sense are interrelational, and intertextual (Wodak and Meyer 2009); that is, they are bigger than individual texts or speakers. It is worth considering different ways of grouping the items/objects that have been accumulated. There is always going to be more than one way of looking at them, but there may be a best way in relation to your particular topic of study. There may also be a way which aligns best with other literature on the topic (not necessarily literature from the CDA approach), which might affect the choice which a researcher makes in terms of their final choice of discourses. All of the researchers whose work makes up the case examples in this chapter acknowledge the interpretational nature of their analysis.

To use case example 4.3 to illustrate this process: the researchers first established their data set, in choosing a specific textbook with a justified reasoning behind that choice. They then read through the chapters repeatedly to familiarize themselves with the data set. Their research questions guided them in what they noticed, which were incidences of content which referred to the relationship between humans and their environment. In their particular case they used a clause-level micro analysis of grammar to consider how those discourses were constructed, and then they grouped them into themes which they used to present the data, such as 'Obfuscating Human Agency in Human-Nature Interactions'.

Positionality

As the process is such an interpretative one, the identity of the researchers is an important influence on the ways in which it is carried out and the outcomes which emerge (even more so than in other forms of qualitative research). Positionality refers to the researcher's position in relation to the topic to be studied and the data that they have collected (or the participants in their study). A 'critical' view must also be turned on ourselves when we undertake such research. Political leanings, personal investment in the classroom, beliefs and past experiences can all colour how we act on the data to come to an interpretation. Trustworthiness is a key concern for qualitative research; we gain it by being honest, clear and transparent in our intentions and relations with the data. In case example 4.1, for example, Emery is clear about his former position as a policy actor and indeed advocate within the implementation of SEL in England and Wales, and how gaining admittance to a university and the world of critical education research changed his viewpoint and his relation to his former world. Wodak refers to this as a requirement for research not to be reproducible (as we might require in quantitative or experimental research) but to be 'retroductable' (2014: 303). This is a translation of a German term *nachwollziehbar*, and means that 'analyses must be transparent, selections and interpretations justified, and value positions made explicit' (Wodak 2014: 312). In this way we can trace backwards the procedures which led to a research finding based on CDA and decide on its trustworthiness for ourselves.

Case example 4.4 illustrates one way in which the position of the researcher can always be key, in that it is written by a teacher-researcher using CDA to understand her own practice. Although the topic itself is not one that challenges power, the context of the power relationships and the social complexities of the classroom led the researcher to choose CDA as the best approach.

Case example 4.4:

'Genre means ... ': a CDA of fourth-grade talk about genre (Schaenen 2010)

Context: An action research study of integrating genre theory teaching into a writing enrichment programme.

Goal: To examine the ways in which genre is successfully and unsuccessfully constructed by fourth-grade students (9–10 years old) in the context of teacher–student discourse.

Outcomes: Initial teacher-led constructions of genre were superficial and avoided the recognition of complexity. A complex student-to-student class discussion, however, enabled the students to work towards an acceptable understanding of the term. Exemplars drawn from the students' home language practices were most useful in exemplifying the term.

Methods: The study utilized video recordings of classroom talk about genre and one-on-one conversations with students who had reviewed post-performance feedback interviews from a genre task undertaken ten months previously. The study is described as action research by the author, but might more readily fall into the category of practitioner research; in any case the goal was to improve teaching and learning by analysing the classroom talk to 'try to make sense of the students' understanding of what I thought I had taught them' (2010: 32). CDA was used given the complicated classroom dynamics and the need to understand how students were constructing the concept of genre for themselves.

Antaki et al. (2003) identify six shortcomings common in wider discourse analysis research. Among them are 'under-analysis by taking sides', which has clear links to positionality, but also 'under-analysis through over-quotation or through isolated quotation' (2003: n.p.), which demonstrates how it is possible to bias the outcome of research through the data which you choose to provide to the reader. Research submitted for publication in academic journals will go through a review process which will (hopefully!) pick up such faults, perhaps even be over-sensitive to them, but it is important for research which is done in other contexts, perhaps for no other audience than within the school in which it is based, to consider these issues even more carefully.

Hallidayan Functional Linguistics

Some CDA (such as case example 4.3) uses very close linguistic analysis to demonstrate the mechanisms by which the discourses are constructed. Michael Halliday's theory of systemic functional linguistics emphasized the meaning-making aspects of language, reflected in the options that were open to, and taken by, people. This concept of choice is central as to why Hallidayan Functional Linguistics is seen as such a useful approach for CDA. If a speaker chooses (as in case example 4.3) the passive voice, then that choice obscures the actor from the audience with particular effect. Some of the options are always available; in other cases options are limited by the context. While some CDA researchers are experts in Halliday, it is always possible to consider the particular grammatical, syntactical and lexical choices made by speakers and writers and to consider why those choices were made and how they affect social reality (e.g. by substituting another choice and seeing how the effect is changed).

Conclusions

There are many different ways to do CDA. We have presented one way in which you might do it, and the case examples demonstrate some other variations on that theme. The main concern of CDA is to bring together linguistic analysis with concerns with social realities, particularly where there are injustices or imbalances in power. CDA gives us the tools to challenge received wisdom and to highlight the construction of particular stereotypes and ideologies through language.

If you are interested in pursuing this line further, it is worthwhile thinking through the particular critical angle that you wish to take, and which critical theory is informing your stance. For each of them you will need to do some reading in the theoretical background *as well as* in the topic of your study; that is for a Foucauldian CDA of school food you need to read Foucault on power as well as a range of different research on school food, not just that which takes the same theoretical and methodological approach. More than most CDA requires the researcher to be well versed in the political, social and research context of the topic, because all of these can be part of the ways in which discourses are constructed in written and spoken language.

Further reading

Rogers, R., E. Malancharuvil-Berkes, M. Mosley, D. Hui and G. O. G. Joseph (2005), 'Critical discourse analysis: A review of the literature', *Review of Educational Research*, 75 (3): 365–415. http://dx.doi.org/10.3102/00346543075003365. This is an authoritative survey of the field of CDA in education at the time which has not been bettered since.

Saldaña, J. (2015), *The coding manual for qualitative researchers*, London: SAGE. This is a general book on the coding process in data analysis, a topic which is not covered in this book more widely, although this chapter touches on it in relation to CDA.

Wodak, R. (2013), *Critical discourse analysis*, London: SAGE. This is an authoritative and comprehensive look at the different approaches to CDA underpinned by strong theoretical material.

CHAPTER FIVE

Sociolinguistics

Introduction

This chapter draws on the use of analysis of discourse to examine sociological issues, and the ways in which the social and cultural aspects of the classroom affect the language used within it. Sociolinguistics is a discipline of linguistics which recognizes the influence that social factors, such as age, gender, region, class and many others, have on the language of the individual. It also considers the ways in which language is utilized to develop and maintain social relationships. This chapter will consider some of the basic tools and terms used in sociolinguistics and then consider some of the many different social contexts which can be of interest to the sociolinguist.

Descriptive linguistics

Sociolinguistics is a branch of descriptive linguistics. It does not prescribe right or wrong forms of language but rather describes what is present. It does, however, concern itself with those who prescribe and what they prescribe, things which are of great interest to those who consider how language relates to the social world. It is this descriptive nature which primarily distinguishes the social concerns of sociolinguistics from the social concerns of CDA which we discussed in the previous chapter. Sociolinguistics is interested in the ways in which language is produced in a social context, rather than with critiquing the power and social constructions that result.

Any features of language can be considered in relation to their social origin. A sociolinguistic analysis of classroom talk or a written document might include the following: the register in which the speaker is operating; the grammatical structures which they use; the lexis which they use; dialect variations on lexis; pronunciation of specific sounds or words; the ways in which they defer or not to other speakers; the paralinguistic features or any one of a number of other tiny variations in the content, production and reception of a linguistic utterance.

Breaking the rules

As we showed in Chapter 2, the unspoken rules of conversation are quite strongly felt and understood by participants in those conversations. Sociolinguistics is often interested in the underlying rules of interaction, albeit in a less technical and more social way than CA. The easiest place to see what the rules are, however, is always to see them being broken. In the previous chapter we gave the example of a teacher being called 'mate' by a pupil. Similarly, imagine someone getting to their feet in a national senate or parliament and swearing roundly in a series of four letter words. These examples demonstrate how violating norms shows us what the norms are. These can be the rules of turn-taking, or who gets to speak. They can also be the norms of how you refer to students, the lexis used in a classroom or the wording of feedback which is given on classwork. When rules or norms are violated but there are no repercussions suggests something interesting is underlying the exchange; in other words, the norm is not violated because other rules are at play. For example, you would be unlikely to call a student an idiot, but you might in certain circumstances where you had a strong and close relationship with that student, where that student would understand you to be joking, and where the context was not school work but an egregious and contextually funny mistake.

Idiolect, dialect, sociolect

The suffix 'lect' relates to speaking; it denotes a language or a language cluster. Most people are familiar with the term 'dialect' which means the language form specific to a certain area. A sociolect is similarly a language form specific to a group of people linked by social class. An idiolect is the form of language particular to an individual. It is formed by the combination of influence from their class, their gender, their nationality, their ethnicity, their family background, their life experiences, their education and their interests as well as potential influences from other characteristics.

Standard English and other dialects

Great emphasis is placed in the English National Curriculum (Department of Education 2014) on learning to speak in 'Standard English'. This is framed in the context of full participation within society: 'pupils who do not learn to speak, read and write fluently and confidently are effectively disenfranchised' (n.p.). It is generally presented in curriculum documents as the 'correct' form of English, but it is itself a dialect; it is whichever dialect is used as the national norm in an English-speaking country. In England and Wales it is associated with the Received Pronunciation accent, although recently it has become more closely related to Estuary English. General American and General Australian English are the equivalents in the United States and in Australia, respectively.

While children are expected to learn their national variant of Standard English through school, and are often taught that it is the only socially acceptable variant that they should speak on all educational and work occasions, almost all of them bring other dialects into the classroom, as do many teachers. If the dialect matches the location of the classroom, this is often unremarkable, but it can become remarkable if the dialect of the teacher differs substantially from that of the students. Victoria undertook one of her teaching placements as a student teacher in Burnley, in Lancashire in the north of England. The students thought that she must come from London (as opposed to just over the border in Yorkshire), because she spoke with a Received Pronunciation accent.

Sometimes specific vocabulary items can be interesting markers of dialectal regional variation. The word for a roll made of bread in England, for example, is variously bap, bread bun, bread cake, barm, barmcake, bread roll, batch or cob. A book with map visualizations of the incidence of different pronunciations and variations of vocabulary items across the United States introduced us to the fact that a miniature lobster of the type usually known as the crayfish or the crawfish is also known as the 'crawdad' in some regions of the United States (Katz 2016).

Dialectal variations can be a source of interest, but they also have the potential to be a source of problems for school children, particularly if the dialect is marked by others as particularly undesirable. In some school situations use of dialect is considered by teachers and therefore other students to be a marker of lower ability, or lower social status. This can obviously have material effects for those students. Individuals may also choose to deliberately maintain their dialect or regional accent within the formal setting of the classroom; considering how and why such a choice is made is also of interest to sociolinguists.

Codeswitching

Codeswitching is a term generally used in studies of bilingualism or English as a Foreign Language to refer to the rapid switching between languages within the speech of a single individual (see Chapter 8 for further discussion of this and the related term 'translanguaging'). However, it can also refer to the switching between different forms of a single language within an individual's range. Students (and teachers) can choose to move between Standard English, their own dialect, a perceived 'youth speak', African American Vernacular English (AAVE) (see below) and others, as they deem appropriate within a conversation. The factors which influence such choices include who the audience is and what the context is. Children can also be quite sophisticated code-switchers, utilizing inappropriate forms deliberately in order to cause an effect, such as laughter (which often results from the unexpected juxtaposition of different registers), or annoyance on the part of the teacher (by producing the undesired form).

Slang and txt lng

Codeswitching is particularly prevalent among young people in relation to 'text language', that is, the set of abbreviations and emojis that constitutes the normal form of communication via text message and internet messaging. Despite the moral panic promulgated by various conservative media outlets, researchers have shown that children are highly alert to the differences between text language and Standard English, and adept at switching between the two. There are constant rumours of an examination script written entirely in text language by a sixteen-year-old in England, but no investigation by any of the Awarding Bodies who set and examine these qualifications has ever been able to turn up such a script. Indeed, research by Wood et al. (2011) showed that the use of text language improved children's phonological awareness and helped them to be able to spell. In any case, the increased availability of predictive text has meant that text language is not so prevalent as it once was (and is indeed often seen as a marker of a middle-aged user of the internet rather than a teenager).

The use of text language, and also of slang, brings us to an interesting aspect of language for sociolinguists: the use of language to signal in-group and out-group behaviour and to establish solidarity between individuals. A phenomenon known as 'accommodation' is the tendency of individuals to converge (or diverge) their speech patterns from those of the person they are talking with. It is the linguistic equivalent of mirroring body language (or the opposite). The use of slang is closely correlated to this, in that its use can display membership of a particular group to other members of that group, and to others outside the group. Using the slang or vernacular of a group to which you do not belong can result in problems if the group does not accept you as their own. Two easy examples of this in education are age-related slang and interest-related slang. To illustrate the former in 2018 one could use the word 'fam' (a piece of slang meaning someone you consider to be part of your family, usually metaphorically). Where teenagers and those in their early twenties can use this without irony, for a teacher to use it in a classroom in an attempt to ingratiate themselves into an in-group would likely lead to ridicule. Interest-related slang might be terminology belonging to an MMO (massive multiplayer online game) or another gaming context; unless you are part of the community it would be very difficult to utilize its slang to a member of it. Neither of us are gamers so we would not attempt to use the word 'pwned' (originating from a mis-typing of 'owned', this is pronounced 'poned'). This kind of in-group marker is characterized by rapid change so that if we were writing this book in two years time we would use different examples (so we ask your forgiveness if 'fam' and 'pwned' are now either completely archaic or so widespread as to be poor examples).

While identifying and categorizing the slang used by students can be an entertaining and instructive research exercise, there is a cautionary tale arising from being over-credulous in this area. When a *New York Times* reporter wanted the 'code' that was associated with the grunge subculture, his insistence that such slang must exist led a young sales representative to invent a lexicon which was printed in the newspaper (Marin 1992). Terms included 'swinging on the flippity flop' to mean hanging out and 'wack slacks' to describe old ripped jeans. This in many ways illustrates the strength of using naturally occurring data to investigate phenomena rather than directly asking people; what is really in use may differ from what they say they use.

AAVE and other ethnic vernaculars

Akin to the use of slang to mark in-group individuals or dialectal variation is the existence of ethnic vernaculars and variations in language. One particular variation which has received a great deal of attention in recent years is AAVE, a vernacular which shares many features with various dialects of the southern United States. This variation in particular receives intense criticism from conservative prescriptivists, to a greater extent than dialects do, which suggests that there is at least an element of racism at work in the attitudes towards AAVE. The use of non-standard dialects and vernaculars is sometimes treated as a marker of a lower level of education. However, speakers who utilize AAVE are just as likely to be making a deliberate choice to express and maintain culture and solidarity as other users of in-group variant vocabulary and structures. AAVE has also made an entrance into youth culture more widely, both inside and outside the United States, possibly via the medium of hip-hop music. It therefore has the potential to be used within classrooms across the English-speaking world, and is utilized as part of a deliberate language profile choice on the part of young people who are constructing particular linguistic identities. This use is not unproblematic. The teacher-researcher in case example 4.4 remarked on her deliberate use of features of Black English to engage her class, namely call and response (Schaenen 2010). The strategy of using AAVE or other ethnic vernaculars in the classroom is one which would be a fruitful topic of sociolinguistic investigation into classroom discourse. AAVE itself is a matter of some controversy, both in terms of its origins and its use, and we would recommend careful reading around the political and social contexts of this variation if you are going to make it a topic of research.

Language and gender

Although the field has largely moved on to consider gender as a performative characteristic, which is constructed and displayed through language choices (Butler 1990), there are long-standing stereotypes of gendered language which are still prevalent among non-sociolinguists. Male language traits are supposed to include interruptions; an avoidance of personal or emotional content; and more direct commands or criticism. Women, on the other hand, are supposed to be more likely to use hedges, tag questions, be polite and to be unassertive (Cameron 2007; Holmes 2006; see also case example 5.1). These stereotypes are made popular by books such as *Men Are from Mars; Women Are from Venus* (Gray 2002), and by careers advice for women that counsels them to change their linguistic strategies to be more masculine. There is even a plug-in for Google mail (Just Not Sorry) that will highlight the use of 'feminine' language such as 'just' and 'sorry' in order to enable women to be more assertive in their email writing.

The more contemporary view is that both men and women adjust their linguistic strategies actively to build and maintain a gendered identity, although there remain no more appropriate terms than 'feminine' and 'masculine' to label the two sets of linguistic strategies (McDowell and Klattenberg 2018). They can also use the opposite style if it is more appropriate to their surrounding context, such as in gendered work roles. Case example 5.1 explores this in relation to primary school teachers in Germany and the UK in relation to their disciplining strategies. By showing the ways in which male teachers enact discipline through typically feminine linguistic strategies, such as using tag questions or positive politeness moves, the authors challenge the idea that gender is the most salient characteristic in interpreting linguistic behaviour. In this case the occupational context is far more important.

Case example 5.1:

Does gender matter? A cross-national investigation of primary classroom discipline (McDowell and Klattenberg 2018)

Context: A study of eight male and eight female teachers from primary school classrooms in the UK and Germany in the context of an extreme shortage of male primary teachers in both countries and a call for more male 'role models' to increase boys' academic attainment.

Goal: To examine men's linguistic behaviour in the classroom in relation to enacting discipline to answer the question: Does teacher gender matter?

Outcomes: All teachers used a mix of linguistic strategies which might be considered typically feminine or masculine, for similar purposes to each other. They constantly shifted strategies in order to use whatever worked best for the individual pupil with whom they were dealing. Some men used typically feminine language, such as tag questions, and hedges, to mitigate the authority of their disciplining, while women used unmitigated, direct discipline. The authors conclude that their finding is aligned with previous studies which suggest that the construction of an occupational role is more important than gendered identity when deploying linguistic strategies; that is, that men will utilize 'feminine' speech styles in a stereotypically feminine job and vice versa. The researchers argue that there is a need to stress occupational competencies rather than 'role model arguments' (p.15) (such as male teachers provide stronger discipline) in order to improve recruitment of men to the profession.

Methods: Sixteen teachers, split equally between male and female, and between Germany and the UK, were audio- and video-recorded. Approximately 160 hours data were transcribed for analysis. Analysis focused on disciplinary strategies employed by the teachers because these are closely linked to gender stereotypes. Linguistic features and their functions were categorized and a comparative analysis between participants enabled the researchers to identify patterns of similarities and differences.

Gendered language *is* found in another context though: the ways that men and women are portrayed implicitly and treated linguistically by the media and other national discourses. Spolsky (1998) points out that the use of the generic masculine (where 'man' stands for 'human'; chairman for chairperson, 'he' is the generic pronoun etc.) reinforces the secondary status of women in many social groups, no matter what the intention of the speaker. Pillay and Maistry (2018) exemplify this in their analysis of the 'firstness' of male pronouns and words in Business Studies textbooks in a range of Southern African countries, where the male part of a collocation such as 'husband and wife' or 'brother and sister' always came first.

Textbooks and the phrasing of science and maths problems are popular topics for looking at gendered language as part of classroom discourse. But students themselves may be reproducing stereotypes through gendered language behaviour (including allowing male students to dominate topic control and turn-taking, given that the teenage years are ones when performance of identity, including gender, becomes extremely important). When Victoria was a young teacher her class of seventeen-year-olds told her (despite her arguments to the contrary about their classroom interactions) that they were past sexism and that their language was that of equality. In the same class a week later one of the boys made a joke about getting the girls to wash up in the sixth form common room because it was a mess, and they all, boys and girls, laughed. A sociolinguistic analysis of gender and language of the classroom interaction of those students would potentially have revealed something very uncomfortable about them to themselves.

Language and power

Apart from the use of a specific dialect form or accent which marks a high socio-economic status and which is not regionally located, there are many other ways in which social status can be marked through linguistic choices. Topic control is one: the right to determine which way a conversation is going is largely given to the most powerful person within that conversation. Power can be fought over in relation to topic control, as any teacher who has ever had a student trying to derail their lesson via a digression will understand. It is also demonstrated through strategies such as interruption. In contrast, the less powerful will utilize strategies such as politeness markers or hedging to ameliorate their communication to the more powerful.

Power becomes an issue not only in relation to teachers and students when it comes to education but also in relation to families. Case example 5.2 demonstrates how family dinner talk can affect the ways in which children are prepared for classroom interaction; in one case Heller relates one parent dominates the dinner table talk and prevents the child from gaining experience as a primary speaker which has consequences for their later classroom interaction.

Case example 5.2:

Discursive practices in family dinner talk and classroom discourse: a contextual comparison (Heller 2014)

Context: A study of naturally occurring data from eleven children in different contexts before and after school enrolment.

Goal: To explore the difference between the discursive practices of the same children in family dinner talk and classroom interaction through micro-analytic analysis of a single genre of talk, namely argumentation.

Outcomes: Children's discursive practices are socially constructed in the different contexts in which they find themselves. Different patterns of talk at home over the dinner table prepare the children for different sorts of interactions: the researcher describes one pattern which is essentially concerned with what is happening at the time at the table, in which the child does not get many opportunities to operate as the primary speaker, and another in which talk is more varied and wide-ranging, with more interaction between all members of the family. In the context of the classroom, the former child is less well prepared to draw on interlocutionary cues offered by the teacher inviting him to repair the statement he has made. The latter has the conversational ability to 'match' the expectations of his teacher. The researcher suggests it is important for teachers to support students to partake in classroom interactions and not to assume that they have the background for successful participation in interaction within the context of the classroom.

Methods: The researchers drew on twenty-five hours of dinner talk and twenty hours of lessons in German primary schools featuring the same eleven children. They used close analysis of segments of talk which demonstrate argumentation to explore how the interlocutors established contexts for argumentation and to establish what interactive patterns appeared. Different contexts were used to comparatively establish the particular features of the teacher–student interactions. This article presents just four sequences which were selected for their representativeness of the corpus.

Typically both parents and teachers are in a position to dictate what is correct and incorrect relative to children. The transcription in Table 5.1 is of a parent–child interaction.

The power relationship is clear to see through the temporal ordering of the activities which the mother suggests, with a reward coming after the more functional activities. She uses the future tense to demonstrate her certainty of what is going to happen. Harry, the child, on the other hand, uses a louder voice to assert what he wants (a bath by himself) but then thanks his mother when she

Table 5.1 Parent–child interaction

1.	Mother	Oohkay	*Lifting finger, gaze towards Harry*
2.		We're gonna get in the bath,	*Still gazing towards Harry*
3.		(0.6)	
4.	Harry	BY MYSELF	
5.	Mother	Yes	
6.		(0.3)	
7.	Harry	Thank you	
8.	Mother	So let me get you in (.) and then after you're	
	Harry	Uh	
9.	Mother	Going to brush your teeth and then we will read a book (.)	
10.	Harry	YESS	

confirms that Harry will be allowed this. Close analysis of linguistic and grammatical features linked with social contextual knowledge is what characterizes sociolinguistic analysis. In this it differs from CA, as discussed in Chapter 2, because CA considers only what the speakers make relevant to the interaction.

Face

The concept of 'face' was introduced into sociology by Erving Goffman in the 1950s (Goffman 1955). The saying 'to save face' exemplifies its meaning: face is the self-image which we present to the world. Part of normal social interaction is to help people preserve face, that is, to work with them cooperatively to accept their 'face value' statements. We are emotionally invested in our face, so that if it is maintained we are happy, and if it is not maintained then that can cause upset. Politeness moves in conversation are fundamentally about helping to preserve face. On the other hand, you can make face-challenging moves in conversation, such as by refusing to believe someone, or asking them to present their evidence or acting impolitely to someone who should be deferred to. Again, it is easy to think of examples of face-challenging language in the classroom in relation to behavioural issues; if a student, for example, says 'that's wrong' in response to a teacher statement without hedging language, that is a face-challenging act. The teacher will then act to recover face – both linguistically and by using disciplinary measures if appropriate. Doing 'facework', that is using linguistic and other strategies to uphold and promote the self-image you have of yourself, is something which all humans engage in, at all times. This means it provides an interesting framework for looking at classroom communication.

Case example 5.3 (Kerssen-Griep et al. 2008) explores face in a particularly face-threatening environment: the giving and receiving of feedback. Their study was a statistical correlation of how students perceived the quality of facework their teachers did when giving feedback and how they perceived the classroom environment on various measures and how they rated the mentorship relationship from their teachers.

Case example 5.3:

Attentive facework during instructional feedback: key to perceiving mentorship and an optimal learning environment (Kerssen-Griep et al. 2008)

Context: A study of linguistic strategies used to give feedback to university students in the United States about their public speaking.

Goal: To investigate the links between face threat mitigation strategies given during feedback and students' judgements of the mentoring relationship with their teachers and the supportiveness of their classroom environment.

Outcomes: Skilled facework on the part of the teachers had a significant impact on how students perceived the supportiveness of the environment and of their teachers. They felt mentored more when facework was done to mitigate the face-threatening possibilities of feedback, and they also felt more satisfied with the mentoring relationship and with the classroom environment, particularly as they related to teacher support in the classroom. As expected, the quality of facework did not predict how students felt about structural aspects, such as the orderliness of the classroom. The authors conclude that working to address face needs is key to providing empowering feedback over time and for how that feedback works to create a classroom environment and teacher–student relationship.

Methods: This was a survey study which asked participants to rate their agreement with items expressed as statements on measures of facework in feedback, mentorship and classroom environment. The participants were 345 undergraduate students enrolled in 27 public-speaking classes in 3 different universities. Public speaking was selected because the researchers thought that 'students' feelings of personal involvement in their evaluated speech performances would create regular face-relevant, potentially ego-threatening feedback situations' (p. 318). They used self-report measures of facework because it enabled participants to report how they had experienced the feedback, no matter what the external perception of the facework done with that feedback was. Confirmatory factor analysis and other statistical analyses were done to confirm the correlations between students' responses on different measures.

Although Kerssen-Griep and colleagues chose the context of a university public-speaking class because they saw it as an example of a particularly face-threatening situation since students are often personally invested in their public speaking, there are plenty of opportunities for face-threatening situations in relation to feedback in education more generally. Brown and Levinson (1987) identified two different needs in relation to face: positive face, which is the need to be socially affirmed by others whose opinion you value; and negative face, which is the need to be free from constraints. The possible threat from feedback is clear: it can be critical and it usually impinges on your ability to do as you wish with a piece of work by imposing further direction or constraint. Critical feedback does not need to be face-threatening, however: by couching it correctly, acknowledging competence and presenting feedback as part of an alliance between teacher and student, feedback can be given without damaging face.

Writing and sociolinguistics: The digital age

Classrooms are interesting places in terms of the sociolinguistics of writing. They are locations where a lot of writing happens, but where much of it is not authentic; that it is produced for another purpose other than its ostensible one. A newspaper article about the Cuban missile crisis in a history classroom is really produced to rehearse and demonstrate historical knowledge, not to inform an audience about contemporary events. A letter to persuade the headteacher to allow the leaving class to hold a prom is really intended to show off rhetorical techniques and mastery of grammar, spelling and punctuation. Even where the task is authentic, such as when students are taking notes for their own later revision, the writing is likely to be influenced by social structures around them: school rules prohibiting pencil, or mandating double underlining, for example.

The digital age has produced many more social contexts where writing may take place and which can be the subject of sociolinguistic analysis. Facebook, Twitter, chatrooms, virtual learning environments and others provide fora where written language is the medium, but with a strong bent towards the kind of instant communication, and the level of formality, which is more normally found in spoken language. In addition the normal social constraints applicable to spoken language which are produced by speaking to someone face-to-face are removed, which can lead to rapid and ill-judged utterances. There is a sense in which the consequences of speaking are removed; individual restraint is lessened by the protection of being behind a keyboard (see Hardaker 2015). At the same time, the consequences can actually be longer reaching, as an individual's digital footprint can be preserved for posterity – or the opposite.

Conclusion

In this chapter we have explored a number of different concepts and terms from sociolinguistics that illustrate the range of possible approaches to classroom discourse data that could be taken within this field. Sociolinguistics can be a particularly rich theoretical approach for working with classroom discourse because classrooms are naturally social settings and the relationships between teachers and students, and between students and students, are played out on through linguistic means. This can only be a brief introduction to the concepts of sociolinguistics and each of these fields has a large literature of its own, which would be worth investigating if one of these areas is of particular relevance. Some of them, such as AAVE, can be controversial and require careful ethical thought (see Chapter 11 for such considerations). Sociolinguistics is also an area where analysis of your own linguistic behaviour can be fruitful, if difficult, because it is not always easy to see our own underlying assumptions laid bare.

Further Reading

Deckert, S. K. and C. H. Vickers (2011), *An introduction to sociolinguistics: Society and identity*, London: Continuum. This is a clear and well-written book which comprehensively introduces the key theoretical concepts of sociolinguistics.

Lillis, T. (2013), *Sociolinguistics of writing*, Edinburgh: Edinburgh University Press. Specifically aimed at those wanting to analyse written texts with a strong theoretical underpinning.

Spolsky, B. (1998), *Sociolinguistics*, Oxford: Oxford University Press. This is a brief introduction to a wide range of concepts and ideas in sociolinguistics: a useful first starting point.

CHAPTER SIX

Corpus Linguistics and Other Quantitative Approaches

Introduction

This chapter largely focuses on corpus linguistics as it is used in the analysis of classroom discourse. At the end of this chapter we also consider other quantitative approaches to analysing classroom discourse, but the sheer scale of this type of research makes it less accessible or manageable by the lone researcher. The analysis also often requires substantial statistical knowledge which is beyond the scope of this book.

Corpus linguistics is often associated with the image of a linguist sitting at a computer trawling through computer-generated lists of words or phrases, with little relevance to classrooms or classroom-based research. However, this is just one part of corpus linguistic research. A corpus is a large database of transcripts or texts that are connected in some way. Educational research involving corpora includes the design and creation of corpora, including those of classroom interactions, and the analysis of corpora of classroom interactions or classroom texts to identify feature of language that are relevant to teaching and learning, as well as researching the use of corpora by students themselves as they learn a language.

Corpus linguistics is a quantitative approach to studying classroom discourse which marks it out as different to all the other approaches we have considered in this book. Within educational research it is often combined with other approaches such as CA or sociolinguistics by using corpus analysis tools to identify linguistic features of classroom discourse which are then studied in more depth using other qualitative approaches. The real strength of corpus linguistics is its use in relating an individual or specific use of a word or phrase to the wider social context within which it was used. Many studies of classroom discourse use a corpus, but to use corpus linguistics they must include the quantitative aspects, such as keyness, concordances or collocations, described below.

Corpora can vary in size with specialized oral or multi-modal corpora being far smaller (around 60,000 words) than corpora of written texts (millions of words). However, as a general rule, the bigger the corpora, the better (Sinclair 1991). A reference corpus is intended to be representative of language as a whole. Examples include the British National Corpus (BNC, see http://corpus.bbyu. edu/bnc/). Specialized corpora on the other hand are only intended to be representative of the context in which they were collected. Corpora are usually studied using computers, but can also be used for more qualitative analyses. There are now a range of specialist software available for analysing corpora, which are particularly useful for the analysis of the larger corpora. Computers enable us to examine the frequencies of particular words or tokens, or collections of words or phrases. They also enable the study of computer-identified pervasive patterns of speech which can tell you about the discourse you are studying. In particular, frequencies of particular words, or groups of words, can tell you a great deal about what is important in the discourse you are studying. The patterns of speech that are of interest in corpus linguistics are often unnoticed because they are so common or mundane (Biber et al. 2006). Patterns of speech can also be used to identify or characterize hegemonic practices in classrooms.

In this chapter we consider corpus linguistics as a theory of language but also as a tool to analyse language as it is used in classroom discourse research. While there is debate around the nature of corpus linguistics, including whether it is a methodology, a theory or a branch of linguistics, here we focus on its use and application in classroom discourse research (interested readers should see Cheng [2011] for a discussion of these different perspectives). Classroom discourse research that makes use of corpus linguistics can consider both written texts (e.g. textbooks or students' essays) and spoken texts (e.g. transcriptions of classroom interaction). Corpus linguistics describes both the construction or compiling of corpora and the analysis of corpora and we will consider both of these as they relate to classroom discourse in this chapter. In addition, we will also consider classroom discourse research that involves the use of corpora in the teaching and learning process, rather than as a method of research.

Building a corpus

The number of corpora that become available for analysis is increasing all the time, but if you are unable to find one that meets your needs, then you may need to build your own. The design of your corpus will depend upon the questions you are seeking to answer. However, one overarching principle that applies to all corpora is that they must be representative of the language you are investigating. The representativeness of a corpus also affects the size of corpus you will need. There are no rules about the size of corpus other than it needs to be big enough to be representative enough to answer your research questions while also being practical in terms of the constraints on your time and resources. To be representative a corpus must include the full range of variability in the language population it is seeking to represent. Sampling rules which apply to statistical research methods may be of help in achieving this. There are also debates as to whether a corpus must be updated in order to remain representative over time (Hunston 2002).

There are a range of software packages available to use to analyse your data, but each of these will have specific requirements about the formatting and meta-data of the corpus you are collecting, which also need to be considered. Generally, within classroom discourse research the corpus is a by-product of a larger research project rather than the focus of the research in the first place (as in case example 6.1). In this situation you will be adapting and formatting your data to fit the requirements of the corpus software you are using. The particular challenge you will face with data from classroom interactions is that the transcript conventions you need for the main study are likely to differ from those needed to be stored as corpus data. Finally, corpora often include 'mark-up', which is additional information attached to a corpus file. This mark-up can describe the document the data is stored in but often includes annotations of the text itself. One of the most common ways of annotating a corpus is with parts of speech (POS) tags, where each word is labelled according to its grammatical category. If you are intending to build your own corpus, then more advice can be found in *The Routledge Handbook of Corpus Linguistics* (O'Keefe and McCarthy 2010).

If you are planning to build a corpus of spoken texts, then you will find that you will need to face the additional challenge of the messiness of spoken data. It can be difficult to distinguish: when it starts and ends; who the audience is (is the teacher talking to the whole class or an individual student – what do you do when they switch between the two fluidly?); and how to transcribe words such as the choice between writing 'gonna' or 'going to' or between writing 'it's' and 'it is'. For CA research this difference matters, but for grammatical studies you need to decide whether you want to consider these two versions as the same word or as different words. Spoken texts also include a lot of hesitation markers, false starts and sounds that may have meaning but are not recognized words. We deal with some of these issues in the chapter on transcription decisions (Chapter 13).

Academic language has been widely studied using corpus linguistics. The Michigan University MICASE corpus is freely available, large and includes a variety of university-situated spoken texts. These include lectures, dissertation defences (vivas) and meetings among other interactions. There are also several freely available corpora of academic writing in a variety of languages, some of which focus on text books, others of which are a collection of student assignments. Corpora of classroom discourse outside of the university setting are less common and less freely available, possibly because of the challenges in building them.

Analysing a corpus

One common use of corpus linguistics is relevant when the texts we are considering can be treated as a register. A register is a term from sociolinguistics that refers to the study of the way in which language is used within a social context, such as the history classroom (Halliday 1993). Here we can choose to look at the use of particular linguistic features within a register or the difference between two different registers. While other forms of discourse analysis will often identify and describe these linguistic features, corpus linguistics provides some quantitative evidence of these features. Having said this, the analysis and explanation of these patterns is still subject to a researcher's interpretation, which will be influenced by their ideological stance (Baker 2006).

Keywords are words that are unique to or occur more frequently within the corpus you are studying when compared to a reference corpus. Keyness describes more than the frequency of particular words but is more about 'a quality words may have in a given text or set of texts, suggesting that they are important' (Scott and Tribble 2006: 73). The software can also identify sequences of words that frequently occur within the corpus and these are usually called lexical bundles, clusters or n-grams depending upon the software.

Table 6.1 Concordance of the word 'understand' in context

1	to get the question and **understand** it and think about it. and get a method
2	try your best and try and **understand** how far you can get it done, okay. here
3	enough other people can **understand** it yeah? and clear enough.
4	going to be and you can **understand** that it works. you know that
5	setting out, so you can **understand** and follow what you've done.
6	put your hands up if you do **understand** why or you've got an explanation
7	so that's good. everybody **understand** now what we're talking about
8	happy with that. everybody **understand** the difference between one d
9	so um that table, did everyone **understand** the explanation on that table
10	okay that is, does everyone **understand** that idea. yeah

The ways in which words form patterns or collocate are usually of particular interest, as they are in case example 6.1.

Concordancing describes the search for the contexts in which particular words occur. With concordance tools you search for a particular word and the computer will show every occurrence of that word within the text either side of it in the corpus. The software also allows you to see how particular words or phrases are distributed through a corpus as a whole. An example of what the concordance output looks like is given in Table 6.1.

The corpus this concordance comes from consists of transcripts of whole-class interactions from a range of secondary mathematics classrooms that Jenni has collected over many years. We have used AntConc version 3.5.7 (Anthony 2018) for the analysis. In this example the search word was *understand* (which is not a very frequently used word in this corpus) and this word is presented in the centre of each line with the immediate context in which the word is used given by the words either side of it. The cases are sorted here by alphabetical order according to the word immediately to the left of the search word but this is something you can alter. This format is commonly known as KWIC (Key Word in Context).

Another common analysis tool is that of collocation. Words that collocate are words that frequently appear closely together and these can be a marker of cohesion or topic organization with a text. If we look at the collocates of the word *think* in Jenni's corpus, the most frequent words are you, I, it, that and to. We can see here that *you think* appears more than twice as often as *think you* for

Table 6.2 Frequencies of the five most common collocates to think

Rank	Freq	Freq(L)	Freq(R)	Collocate
1	395	275	120	you
2	335	258	77	I
3	191	40	151	it
4	164	40	114	that
5	150	97	53	To

example (i.e. the frequency of *you* before *think* is 275, while the frequency of *you* after *think* is just 120).

A lexical bundle is a frequently occurring set of three or more words identified within a particular corpus (Biber et al. 2006). Different disciplines will have different lexical bundles, which illustrate the different purposes and perspectives of the norms of communication within these different disciplines (Hyland and Hamp-Lyons 2002). The discourse of a higher education classroom will be different from the discourse of an early years classroom and the frequency of the different lexical bundles within these classrooms gives an indication of the nature of these differences.

There are a range of ways to classify lexical bundles. Biber et al. (2006) define lexical bundles that communicate 'personal feelings, attitudes, value judgments, or assessments' (p. 966) as stance bundles. Within this they make a further distinction between personal stance and impersonal stance bundles depending on whether the stance is attributed to a speaker or writer, or not. They also distinguish between epistemic, attitudinal or modality stance bundles which include categories of desires, obligations, intentions and ability. These include phrases such as 'if you want to'. They also identify discourse organizing bundles, referential bundles and special conversational function bundles.

One example of the use of a lexical bundle analysis of classroom discourse is given in case example 6.1. The analysis presented in this case examples builds on the techniques developed by Biber et al. (2004) and the process of the identification of the lexical bundles is described elsewhere (Herbel-Eisenmann et al. 2010). The case example instead focuses on the interpretation and analysis of

Case example 6.1:

Appraising lexical bundles in mathematics classroom discourse: Obligation and choice (Herbel-Eisenmann and Wagner 2010)

Context: The corpus analysed consisted of 148 transcripts of interactions in middle and high school mathematics classrooms in the United States that had been collected by the researchers in other studies. The corpus included data from eight teachers in seven different schools and these teachers and schools were chosen to ensure there was diversity in the contexts in which the teachers and students were working. The observations took place over a year, with data being collected on four separate occasions.

Goals: To illustrate how stance bundles position (Harré and van Langenhove 1999) teachers, students and the discipline of mathematics. In particular the authors sought to identify the different kinds of authority structures within the classrooms and how these might influence the teaching and learning of mathematics.

Outcomes: The lexical bundles within the corpus were almost exclusively spoken by the teachers. The combining of lexical bundle analysis and positioning theory led to the identification of three categories of stances related to authority. These include Personal Authority, where the authority lay with the teacher; Demands of the Discipline as Authority, where the authority lay with the discipline of mathematics; and More Subtle Discursive Authority for situations, where the authority seemed to lie with some presence external to the students. They also identified one further category, Personal Latitude, where the bundle involved some choice, which overlapped with the other categories.

Methods: The transcripts came from classroom observations of eight teachers in seven schools in the United States. The lexical bundles were identified using the Lexical Bundles programme developed by Biber et al. (2004) and a cut-point of forty instances of four-word combinations appearing in five or more classrooms. MonoConcPro (Barlow 2002) was then used to examine the identified bundles within the context in which they appeared. The analysis then focused the stance bundles which were also the most frequently occurring type of lexical bundle in the first stage of the analysis. Positioning theory was then used to frame the analysis of these stance bundles and identify bundles relating to authority, control and power. The authors also used systemic functional linguistics and CDA to classify and interpret the bundles they identified. The researchers also did a member check, taking some of the concordance tables to the teachers whose lessons had been transcribed for their feedback and interpretations.

the identified lexical bundles and their role in terms of authority structures within the mathematics classroom.

One challenge that faces corpus linguists is identifying and analysing broader features of discourse other than word use that are identifiable through the tools discussed above. Identifying the features of a text that makes it cohesive, or how discourse markers such as 'on the other hand' or 'therefore' can be consequential with some disciplines. Researchers within corpus linguistics are continuously working on developing tagging systems or computer packages to overcome these challenges. To analyse the use of discourse markers at the moment you will need to identify which discourse markers to look for within your corpus. Identifying lexical bundles, as discussed above and in case example 6.1, is one way to identify some discourse markers as used by Biber et al. (2004) and Herbel-Eisenmann et al. (2010). Here you need to consider both the frequency of the markers and how they are used. It is this function of the discourse markers that is of interest in educational research and is also where your expertise and familiarity with the context matters.

Case example 6.2 offers an example of how corpus analysis can be complemented with other discourse analysis approaches to look at organizational features of a discourse. The authors use corpus linguistic techniques in the building of the corpus but is not strictly speaking an example of corpus linguistics, as they have not made use of any of the quantitative tools mentioned above. However, they *have* used frameworks developed by other researchers who have drawn upon these tools in the construction of the frameworks.

Case example 6.2:

Analysing teachers' use of metadiscourse: The missing element in classroom discourse analysis (Tang 2017)

Context: Metadiscourse is talk about talk itself. It is used to organize discourse, control the flow and direction and to signal boundaries, but also indicates the speaker's or writer's stance towards both the content and others. It helps us to make connections, interpret and evaluate within the communicative norms in which we are interacting. This paper focuses on the use of metadiscourse by six science teachers in Singapore where English is the medium of instruction.

Goal: To examine the role of metadiscourse in the teaching and learning of science. In particular, to identify the kinds of metadiscourse used by teachers when they interact with students, and how the teachers use metadiscourse to construct scientific knowledge in interaction.

Outcomes: Six categories of metadiscourse were identified: text connective, knowledge connective, activity connective, attitude marker, epistemology maker and interpretative marker.

Methods: The corpus was created through the video recording of six science teachers from three schools collected from two separate research projects. A total of 125 lessons were video recorded and transcribed, and the episodes of whole-class talk were analysed. The analysis was originally based on coding schemes from Chin (2006), Lemke (1990) and Vande Kopple (2012) and included an interaction-discursive, content-semantic and metadiscourse analysis. The metadiscourse analysis began with Vande Kopple's (2012) framework but was refined to suit the nature of the oral discourse within science classrooms.

One of the frequent criticisms of corpus linguistics is that the data it handles is decontextualized. Widdowson argues that because the text being analysed is separated from its original context we cannot consider it to be authentic language (2000). Its decontextualized nature means we have to be careful in the claims we are making about language use. However, more and more specialized corpora are being developed, where the context in which the data is collected and the tight design of the corpus mean that we can make some interpretations of the data in relation to the context, something that is not possible with the larger corpuses, such as the BNC. This is particularly the case if you, as the researcher, are familiar with the sociocultural context in which the data is collected.

In the analysis of classroom discourse we are usually interested in language use. One focus of corpora analyses of classroom discourse has been the use of personal pronouns, both in written texts and in spoken texts. In general, pronouns are used more frequently in language learner's written work than in native speaker's written work (Gilquin et al. 2007). Personal pronouns have both a pragmatic and a psychological aspect: they tell us something about how information or knowledge is being treated as shared or not and also tell us about the social relationships between speakers. Fortanet (2004) looked at the use of the pronoun *we* in university lectures and then later (2006) the use of the pronouns *you* and *I* and found that they are used to refer to a range of people both to those within the interaction and to people not present. Personal pronouns also serve a range of discourse functions. Case example 6.3 illustrates one study that compares the use of personal pronouns in two different corpora.

Case example 6.3:

'You' and 'I' in university seminars and spoken learner discourse (O'Boyle 2014)

Context: The personal pronouns 'you' and 'I' often indicate shared knowledge and mark stance as well as supporting the development and maintenance of relationships between teachers and students. Existing research has shown that there are differences in the ways that experts and novices, native speakers and non-natives speakers use personal pronouns and differences between spoken and written tasks. This study arose out of a concern for the difficulties students in English for Academic Purpose lessons face in participating in classroom interactions.

Goal: To identify similarities and differences in the frequency and nature of use of the personal pronouns *you* and *I* between a corpus of English learner spoken discourse and a corpus of native speaker spoken discourse, both in a classroom setting.

Outcomes: The analysis identifies different patterns in the way 'You' and 'I' are used between the two corpora. Both pronouns appeared in the top ten most frequently occurring words within the corpora, with *you* appearing more frequently than *I* in both corpora. The first key finding was that students use *You* and *I* more frequently than teachers. Another key finding was that there was a higher use of *I* in spoken learner discourse compared to native speaker spoken discourse. The most frequently occurring two-word cluster was *I think,* followed by *I mean* and then *I don't. I think* occurred almost three times more often in the learner corpus than in the native speaker corpus. Similarly, pronoun repetition was far more frequent in the learner corpus than in the native speaker corpus. O'Boyle argues that the differences between the learner corpus and the native speaker corpus could be because the learners focus more on the psychological aspects of language use, whereas native speakers also consider the relational aspect, but also that English learners may draw on a narrower range of discourse markers in their talk, leading to the high frequency of particular word clusters.

Research methods: O'Boyle analyses two corpora of spoken texts, one of English language learners' task talk and the other of university seminar talk. Thus she is comparing spoken discourse from fifteen university classrooms in a range of disciplines with both non-native and native speakers of English to a corpus of adult English language learners completing speaking tasks in an upper-intermediate- or advanced-level classroom context. As the two corpora were different in size, O'Boyle used normalized frequencies of a rate of occurrence per 1000 words. The data was transcribed orthographically and included fillers such as *uh* or *um,* and repetitions such as *you you.* The data was then analysed using the Wordlist and Concordance features of Wordsmith Tools (5.0) (Scott 2008). The frequency lists of the two corpora were compared, including the frequency of occurrence of the words 'you' and 'I' as well as their associated word clusters. The final stage of the analysis was to examine the concordance lines of the words 'you' and 'I' as well as the common word clusters that included these words qualitatively to identify how they were being used.

In this chapter we have focused on the simpler quantitative tools of corpus linguistics but with a large enough corpus there are also a range of statistical methods for identifying keyness or significant differences between different classroom discourse contexts. If this is something you are interested in doing in your own research, then there are a range of books specifically focusing on quantitative corpus linguistics (e.g. Gries 2016).

The use of corpora in language teaching and learning

Recently there has been a shift to considering the pedagogical applications of corpus linguistic research, including by asking students to use the tools of corpus linguistic themselves. There is now a range of curriculum materials that focus on features of both spoken and written discourse that have been developed out of corpus analysis. Concordance lines can be used to enable students to explore how particular words are used within specific contexts. Comparing word use in expert and novice corpora can be used to teach about errors and markers of disfluency. For example, Chambers and O'Sullivan (2004) used error tagging followed by students investigating a corpus when teaching correction and remediation of student writing.

Corpora are now beginning to be used in language education as a way of enabling students to see the regularities of language use within particular contexts. The tools of corpus analysis can offer 'an evidence-based approach to language teaching' (Hyland 2006). However, students will need to develop the skills of investigation associated with corpora analysis. We have only briefly discussed the use of corpora in language teaching, as this is a context for researching classroom discourse, rather than a method of researching classroom discourse; however, there is no reason why you cannot combine the two.

Other quantitative approaches

While corpus linguistics is the most common quantitative way of analysing classroom discourse there are also a range of studies that use coding frameworks in the analysis of classroom observations or videos of teaching practices. The OECD TALIS Video Study involves the collection and analysis of around 170 of videos of teaching practices (2 lessons from around 85 teachers) from each of 8 school systems and aims to explore relationships between teaching practices and student cognitive and non-cognitive outcomes. The study combines data from teacher and student questionnaires, a pre- and post-mathematics test and the analysis of these videos and the accompanying lesson materials. The videos are analysed using a specifically designed coding framework which includes measures of discourse and classroom interaction, such as the nature of questioning and the quality of explanations (OECD 2018).

There are a range of observation schedules available that have been used reliably in a range of countries (Ingram et al. 2018). Those most suitable for the quantitative analysis of classroom discourse are usually found in the field of teacher effectiveness, as these schedules have been developed with validating and reliability in mind; however, using observation schedules necessarily involves a simplification of what can be observed and measured. One such schedule that is widely used in a variety of contexts is the Classroom Assessment Scoring System (CLASS). Case example 6.4 illustrates how this particular schedule can be used to study classroom interaction in a quantitative way.

Case example 6.4:

Impacts of the CARE for Teachers program on teachers' social and emotional competence and classroom interactions (Jennings et al. 2017)

Context: This study took place in a high-poverty region of New York City in the United States and studied 224 teachers from 36 primary schools and the interactions within their classrooms.

Goal: To examine the influence of a mindfulness-based professional development programme (CARE for Teachers) on the quality of classroom interactions.

Outcomes: The results showed that the professional development had a positive effect on the emotional support domain of the CLASS. This domain includes four dimensions: positive climate, negative climate, teacher sensitivity and regard for student perspective. The positive effects were found in positive climate and teacher sensitivity. For the other domains, there was a marginally statistically significant positive effect of the professional development on classroom organization but no effects on the domain of instructional support.

Research methods: A cluster randomized trial design was used, involving 36 primary schools and 224 teachers. Each of the teachers took part in thirty hours of in-person training and personal coaching. The teachers completed online questionnaires of self-report psychological measures and assessments of the students in their class both before and after the professional development. Lesson observations used the CLASS schedule and involved certified raters who also participated in regular calibration meetings. Each teacher was observed twice within the same week for one hour each time. Each observation resulted in a score being allocated every fifteen minutes for each of the three domains of the CLASS, and then averaged across both observations so that each teacher has one score. The analyses then used two-level Hierarchical Linear Models and were performed using MPLUS. For the models of classroom observations covariates of grade level, classroom type, student–teacher ratio, teacher race, proportion of students with SEN, proportion of students ever suspended and teacher perceived average level of support for learning in the home were included.

The quantitative study of classroom interaction often involves considerable sample sizes, and consequently studies usually involve teams of researchers to manage the data collection and analysis. Issues of intercoder reliability, ensuring consistency in ratings both between coders and within coders over time, also need careful consideration.

Conclusion

This chapter has offered a brief introduction to the most common forms of quantitative analyses of classroom discourse, including some of the most commonly used tools within corpus linguistics when they are applied to the analysis of classroom discourse. Other approaches such as CA and CDA are now beginning to make use of corpus linguistics (see O'Keeffe and McCarthy 2010 for a range of examples of this in practice) by automating some of the processes which these approaches can build on. Corpus linguistics itself can only identify the surface-level features of classroom discourse within a particular context. This might explain why in research focusing on classroom discourse, corpus linguistics is used in combination with other approaches. Observational methods using schedules are also being continually developed, including the development of software to transcribe and code classroom interaction – though this is still a long way off achieving the reliability and validity in coding needed at the moment.

Further Reading

Biber, D. (2006), *University language: A corpus-based study of spoken and written registers*, Amsterdam: John Benjamins. A corpus-based description of registers within classroom teaching, office hours, study groups, textbooks and course syllabi.

O'Keeffe, A. and M. McCarthy (2010), *The Routledge handbook of corpus linguistics*, Abingdon, Oxon: Routledge. This book is a useful introduction to the tools of corpus linguistics as well as detailed guidance on how to design your own corpus.

Applications and Topics for Classroom Discourse Research

Introduction to Part Two

These four chapters explore, problematize and exemplify substantive themes in education research which have been studied by using more than one of the approaches considered in Part One. Together they illustrate the diversity of classroom discourse research. In each chapter we consider the frameworks introduced in Part One as they are applied to the themes of identity, multilingual classrooms, knowledge and knowing, and written texts. We compare and contrast the advantages and disadvantages of each approach in the context of specific areas of research, and illustrate the ways in which making a methodological choice is strongly related to the kinds of knowledge and claims that research into classroom discourse can generate.

Chapter 7 examines the very topical area of research, that is identity. This chapter exemplifies the difference between the approaches we explore in Part One and the impact of the different decisions made as a consequence of the approach taken. It explores how the theoretical approach affects the conceptualization of identity/identities. This is a topic which in particular is conceptualized in radically different ways and the approach therefore has fundamental consequences for research design and outcomes. One topic related to identity which we do not explore in much depth is agency, which is another potential key focus for classroom discourse research.

Chapter 8 moves the focus on to the context of multilingual classrooms, teachers and learners. This is a rapidly expanding area of research that draws on a wide range of fields both inside and outside education. This leads to a range of evolving debates about what language is, what it means to be bilingual and pedagogies associated with multilingual learners. This has been an area of research where there has been considerable change in focus and emphasis over the last ten years, to include ideas such as translanguaging and communicative repertoires.

Chapter 9 considers the complexities of knowledge and knowing, which reside at the heart of the educational endeavour. We explore the different ideas about what knowledge is, and how these relate to the different theoretical approaches outlined in Part One, and also to different disciplinary subject traditions. We specifically consider knowledge in relation to the context of classroom discourse; this chapter does not delve into testing or assessment in relation to student knowledge. We reflect on the different evidence bases which can be given as claims for knowledge, and end by taking a critical view of how knowledge can be framed as unproblematic in schools, universities and society at large.

Chapter 10 turns to research using written texts, and explores the opportunities and challenges of using this rich vein of data. The chapter considers the wide range of written texts which are relevant data for researchers in classroom discourse and the ways in which written texts can overlap with or support research using spoken data. We discuss in some detail the questions which may arise if you chose to design your own assessment rubric for written data produced by pupils, and some additional methods of analysis which relate to written texts, such as multimodal analysis.

CHAPTER SEVEN

Researching Identity through Classroom Discourse

Introduction

One area in which researchers have been considering the relationship between the individual and the classroom context is through the idea of identity or identities. Identity can be conceptualized in a multitude of ways, but within the context of research into classroom interaction, it is usually seen as something fluid and dynamic. Identity can change from moment-to-moment as teachers and students interact with each other, and as such is *co-constructed* or is *a joint accomplishment* by the participants in the interaction. Where the different approaches to researching identity differ is in how they consider the relationship between the norms, practices, social, cultural and/or historical contexts in which these interactions occur and people's identity. Some approaches, such as those grounded in ethnomethodology or CA, focus solely on the interaction, others draw upon a wider context and analyse how participants make use of this wider context as they interact, while others still focus on how this wider context influences the interactions themselves. The perspective taken affects how researchers consider the nature of identity, the formation of identities and the evolution of identities in interaction. Are identities formed by joint negotiation within the norms and practices of the classroom? Are identities an outcome of participating in the practices of the classroom? Are identities formed by accepting and adopting these norms and practices?

Within this fluid conceptualization of identity there are still a wide range of ways of researching it. One way to research identity would be to look at how a particular identity is recognized by others within interaction (Gee 1999, 2000). Another way is to look at how individuals describe themselves or position themselves in interaction or particular practices within the classroom (e.g. Solomon 2007). Alternatively, we could study how identities shift as students and teachers participate in particular activities (e.g. Kim and Viesca 2016; Wood 2013). Identity can be treated as either an attribute of an individual or an action, and it is important to consider the distinction carefully as there is a risk of taking a theoretical perspective that treats identities as actions, but then treat the data as demonstrating identities as attributes of an individual. This distinction is most evident in the ways that researchers talk about identities, such as students or teachers doing identity work. The study of identity is also often used to consider issues of power, access and equity. It can also be used to help us to understand why students choose to participate in a particular course, subject or activity.

In this chapter we will examine how each of the theoretical perspectives described in Part One of this book approaches the idea of identity. Alongside these we will also include other perspectives that are drawn upon by researchers examining classroom discourse. Most classroom-based research using the notion of identity has its roots in sociocultural theories, such as Wenger's communities of practice (1999), Holland and colleagues' figured worlds (1998) or Gee's (2000) discourse identities, but draw upon different methodologies including those grounded in ethnomethodology, positioning theory and CDA, as they examine the identities of teachers and students in interaction.

Ethnomethodological approaches to identity

Ethnomethodological approaches to studying identity, such as CA and DP which are discussed in Chapter 2, view identity as something that is accomplished in interaction. They make no attempt to define identity, instead they talk about identity work and focus on what and how participants draw on particular identities as they interact.

Consider the identity of being a teacher. In interaction the title 'teacher' is rarely directly used, so what is it about the interaction that tells us that someone is a teacher (or not)? CA researchers generally describe people as 'orienting to' specific identity categories and they are interested in both how they do this and the consequence this has on the interaction that follows. DP in particular focuses on participants situated descriptions of others, including categories of people. Here the interest is on how social identities are claimed, resisted and used in interaction.

The analysis focuses solely on the structure (e.g. turn-taking, preference organization) and content of the interaction, only taking into account broader contextual aspects if the participants themselves draw upon them in the interaction itself. They do not engage with any pre- or post-theorizing about the social, cultural or political implications of the identity categories oriented to. The identity of teacher is often evident through common modes of address such as Sir or Miss, as well as through the asymmetric speaking rights, different content-specific lexical choices (e.g. the use of technical vocabulary) and different goal orientations of teachers and students. Teacher questions in classrooms also tend to do the action of 'testing' rather than 'information seeking' (Benwell and Stokoe 2006). This focus solely on interactions also extends to any analysis around issues or agency, power or equality. Every person in an interaction can be categorized in a number of ways but it is the identities that are consequential to the participants in the interaction that matters in the analysis. This stance allows for participants to shift identities and potentially draw upon contradictory identities as the interest is on how participants do this.

The notion of identity or identities can also be considered at different levels. In case example 7.1 Sharma draws upon Zimmerman's (1998) ideas of discourse identity, situated identity and transportable identity. Discourse identity refers to those identities used moment-to-moment in an interaction, such as questioner or answerer, expert or novice. Situated identities are those that are associated with the situational context, such as student and teacher (also referred to as default identities [Richards 2006]). Transportable identities are 'usually visible' such as those associated with age, race or gender etc. Here both Zimmerman and Richards are considering identity at three different levels: the level of interaction; the level of the institutional context; and the broader social and cultural contexts in which the individual lives.

Case example 7.1:

Enactment of teacher identity in resolving student disagreements in small group peer interactions (Sharma 2013)

Context: This study took place in an advanced academic writing class with seven international graduate students in the United States. It focuses on how the situational identities (Zimmerman 1998) of teacher and student are oriented to in the classroom interactions.

Goals: To examine a particular challenge students face when working in groups, that of handling disagreements. In particular, Sharma aims to investigate how the identities and roles of teachers and students are negotiated in order to resolve student disagreements when they arise.

Outcomes: Sharma identified two distinct situations where the disagreements among the students were closed and the teacher's situation identity was invoked: where the teacher intervention was invoked by the students, and where the teacher voluntarily intervened. In the first of these cases the students are explicitly treating the teacher as more knowledgeable and in the second case it is the teacher themselves who is treating themselves has having the knowledge and competence to deal with the disagreement. The analysis shows how the unequal distribution of knowledge and language skills available to the teacher and students is used as a strategic device by the 'knowing' party.

Methods: Twelve hours of classroom interactions were video-recorded, where the students worked in two groups on the tasks set. Sharma uses CA to analyse the data. Forty-eight cases of disagreement were identified in these interactions, where disagreements were identified as interactions where different speakers gave oppositional stances or opinions. Sharma then used a sequential analysis to identity two situations where the teacher's situational identity was used to close these disagreements between students.

With any CA-based research, the identity of teacher cannot be assumed, and the analyst can only use this label where the interactional behaviour is that usually associated with a teacher, such as control over topic, asking questions and turn-taking(Richards 2006). In case example 7.1 the identity of teacher is visible in the way both the students and the teacher treat this identity of teacher as one that is more knowledgeable as well as one who offers help and support. However, this is one of the challenges of using ethnomethodological approaches, ensuring that we only make claims based on what can be shown in the data and not making inferences that go beyond this (Ingram 2018).

Membership Categorization Analysis

Another ethnomethodological approach to the study of identities is membership categorization analysis (MCA) (e.g. Sacks 1992; Stokoe 2012). MCA focuses on how participants draw upon categories when they interact, but also in interviews and textual data. The origins for this approach again lie within Harvey Sacks's (1992) lectures on conversation where he outlines the idea of a membership categorization device (MCD). The key example often used to illustrate this is the statement 'The baby cried. The mommy picked it up' (Sacks 1992). Sacks argued that when we read or hear this statement we make links between 'baby' and 'mommy', in particular, that the mommy is the mommy of the baby. He describes the MCD of family as allowing the categories of 'mommy' and 'baby' to be grouped together. These categories are seen as linked to particular actions or characteristics, as well as norms about what constitutes the behaviour of a mummy or daddy. The analysis of interaction then focuses on which categories are used by participants, how participants ascribe, avow and display membership of particular categories (Antaki and Widdicombe 1998). The argument is that 'institutions "think" in terms of categories … and they act on the basis of categories to pursue their tasks' (Mäkitalo and Säljö 2002: 59). This approach to studying identity is becoming more popular in a range of fields, particularly in medical research, and sociological studies, including those of adolescence. However, as it is largely based on the analysis of interviews and focus groups within education it is largely used to consider how individual students categorize themselves, rather than in the study of classroom interaction (though see Richards [2006] for an example of MCA in the analysis of classroom interactions).

Each of these ethnomethodological approaches examines language as action within interaction. They challenge the idea that we can take what people say in interviews as sufficient, with identity being something internal to the person this is simply being expressed in language during the interview. In interaction it is not the individual that is the source of identities, but identities are instead a social construction (Potter and Wetherell 1987). It is the interaction that is the unit of analysis not the individual. For discursive psychology 'identity resides in language practices and not "in the head". This is not an argument that there is nothing "in the head", but that what is externalised does not seamlessly map on to some internalised independent structure' (McAvoy 2016: 102).

Figured worlds and positioning theory in identity research

Figured worlds and positioning theory (as introduced in Chapter 3) are probably one of the most widely used theoretical frameworks for studying the construction and negotiation of identities within the classroom. Positioning theory and figured worlds combine the macro- and micro-levels of analysis, with research using positioning theory emphasizing the micro (as in case example 7.2) more than research using figured worlds which generally emphasizes the role of the broader sociocultural context (as in case example 7.3). Here again identities are constituted in talk. Positioning theorists examine how these identities are co-constructed in interaction usually with a focus on social power relations. Similarly to the approaches above, these co-constructed identities and power relations can be resisted, negotiated and accepted, thus allowing for individual agency in this co-construction. Research using positioning theory or figured worlds often also makes use of narrative analysis where the interest is in the stories we tell about ourselves and others. Thus the analysis often draws both from transcripts of classroom interactions and interviews with teachers and students.

Case example 7.2 draws on this notion of figured worlds and develops the idea of a performative identity to describe how students construct their interactions during group work in science lessons.

Case example 7.2:

Performative identity as a resource for classroom participation: Scientific Shane vs. Jimmy Neutron (Anderson and Zuiker 2010).

Context: The study was a two-year evaluation project of three technology-enhanced learning environments. The students discussed in this paper were part of an elective biology class in a US high school in one of these technology-enhanced learning environments. This broader study included a pre–post learning measures and the incorporation of formative assessment activities developed by the research team.

Goal: To understand how student learning might be shaped by and evidenced in group participation during group reflection discussions.

Outcomes: In this study the authors develop the idea of performative identity – a persona which the students within the group situate and frame their participation, which enable the students to enact different ways of knowing. For example, one student interactionally positions his competence by voicing his contributions in a marked way, by changing the pace and intonation of his speech to mimic that of someone other than him when he is enacting 'being scientific'. The claim is that this positioning enables the students to engage with the texts and routines of working in group reflection discussions in ways which are not necessarily part of the structure of the task. This analysis particularly exemplifies the relationship between features of the interactional setting and how students' participation positions them within that context.

Methods: The teacher and two groups of students were video recorded during parts of lessons that included what the authors describe as formative feedback activities or group reflection discussions, but the paper focuses on the interactions of just one of these groups. The analysis focused on the transcriptions of the video recordings and focused on epistemic and affective knowledge claims, scientific argumentation and 'I' and 'you' statements. The analysis was conducted at three levels. First, a personal participation trajectory is identified for each of the students and the teacher involved. Then there is a narrative description of the collective group dynamics. Finally, there was a micro-interactional analysis of the group interactions.

Both case examples 7.2 and 7.3 explore the relationship between students' identities and particular curriculum areas. Case example 7.2 in particular focuses on what it means to have a scientific identity, and how this meaning is negotiated, accepted and rejected by students. In contrast, case example 7.3 explores how the broader storyline of ability or disability, alongside different pedagogic practices, can influence what it means to be a good student in mathematics.

The concept of figured worlds has been widely used in research examining identity in relation to the community of the classroom or the activities of the classroom. Like positioning theory, figured worlds focus on how individuals both perform and narrate stories about themselves and others in relation to the broader storylines. Both teachers and students use the storylines associated with the classroom when interacting with each other, but can also use these storylines to develop other storylines. These storylines carry particular obligations and entitlements for the teachers and students who are recruiting them through their interactions (Harré and van Langenhove 1999).

One such popular storyline is that of the 'achievement gap', where distinctions are made between the educational achievements of students from different races, gender or social background (e.g. Esmonde 2009). This storyline can lead to students being categorized in particular ways, such as disengaged, fast worker and underachieving. Case example 7.3 illustrates this idea of storyline by exploring the storyline of ability and disability and how it affects students' experiences of mathematics. Lambert (2015) focuses on how the positioning of two students as able or disabled changes during the course of year in school. Here the author draws upon both classroom interactions and interviews to examine both how the two teachers position the students and how the students position themselves.

Case example 7.3:

Constructing and resisting disability in mathematics classrooms: a case study exploring the impact of different pedagogies (Lambert 2015)

Context: The ethnographic study was based in a US middle school and focused on twelve students, chosen based on their gender and prior attainment as well as disability status. All of these students identified as Latina/o thought they had different levels of proficiency in Spanish and English. The larger study was longitudinal and followed the students through their sixth and seventh grades.

Goal: To examine how students construct and enact understandings of ability and disability in mathematics over the course of a year. This also included a closer examination of how two particular students with learning disabilities developed understandings of themselves as mathematics learners during this year.

Outcomes: Luis participated eagerly in the discussion-based parts of the lessons. Ana, on the other hand, excelled during the procedural parts of the lesson and the practice of the procedures she was learning. Ana preferred to be shown how to perform procedures, and Luis refused to follow procedures he did not understand. The analysis highlights the multiple, sometimes contradictory, understandings the two students had about themselves as learners. Ana, although successful at mastering the procedures taught towards the end of the year and increasingly positioned by her teachers as able in mathematics, positioned herself as separate from those she saw as good at mathematics. Luis was initially positioned as a 'top' mathematics student when the focus was on open-ended problems and discussion, but became positioned as increasingly disabled when there was a shift to learning procedures which resulted in him being placed in the special education group. The paper also reports on the consequences of the students being labelled as disabled as they were placed in tracked classes, and the 'discourse of care' were used by the special needs teacher to place both students in a support group, despite their abilities within mathematics.

Methods: Lambert observed two twelve-year-old students, Ana and Luis, identified by their school as having learning disabilities in their mathematics lessons for a year. In this class, the teaching style changed through the year, moving from problem-solving and open-ended mathematical discussions to memorizing procedures for the high-stakes tests that the students needed to take at the end of the year. The teachers involved included both a mathematics teacher and a special needs teacher who were also interviewed. The mathematics teacher, Ms. Marquez, consciously split her teaching into types of pedagogy, discussion-based and procedural. Towards the beginning of the year her lessons began with discussion-based activities and then shifted towards procedural, whereas in the second semester the lessons were largely procedural. The special education teacher joined the class in the second semester and worked with a small group of students that included Luis.

The mathematics lessons were observed over the course of the year, field notes taken and some of the lessons were also video recorded and transcribed. The students were also interviewed twice, once at the beginning of the year and once at the end of the second semester. The first interviews were paired interviews while the second interviews were individual, though not all of the foci students consented to being interviewed twice.

The study took the view that ability and disability are constructed through participation in certain practices. The analysis focused on how these two students positioned themselves and were positioned as able and disabled.

Case example 7.3 also illustrates the interrelationship between classroom pedagogies and student identities, but also emphasizes the social construction of these identities over time and the consequences particular classroom experiences have on these developing student identities. This idea of the interrelationships between particular pedagogies or practices and students' identities can offer significant insight into the wider impact of curricula, policy and practice changes that are implemented around the world.

Sociolinguistics and CDA approaches to identity

Within CDA (as introduced in Chapter 4), identity-focused research has aimed to identify existing discourses that are associated with particular institutions or particular practices which operate across a range of contexts. Here, identity is 'about conveying to one another what kind of people we are; which geographical, ethnic, social communities we belong to; where we stand in relation to ethical and moral questions; or where our loyalties are in political terms' (De Fina 2006: 263). CDA approaches to identity have a political agenda around raising awareness about the ideological frameworks and cultural discourses that affect our language choices and how particular individuals may be positioned within the institutional contexts. The focus is not on language use in and for itself, but on the 'linguistic character of social and cultural processes and structures' (Fairclough and Wodak 1997: 271). CDA attempts to link the micro interactional context to the macro discourses by careful analysis of the interactions, within the social–cultural contexts or discourse in which the interaction occurs. As a result of the political agenda and interest in power and ideology, CDA tends to focus its conclusions at the macro level, and to critiquing social practices with the aim of changing them. Discourses that categorize people in particular ways suppress differences and therefore contribute to inequalities, marginalization and exclusion. However, within this perspective while identity is socially constructed, this does not mean that it can be changed through individual action. From a CDA perspective, social structures are both durable and resistant to change as people do not often reflect consciously on its existence (Zotzmann and O'Regan 2016).

Within CDA research, the researcher has a reflexive relationship with the research in that they must take into account their own identity and how this might influence the research. The gender, social and racial identification of the students, the teacher and the research team are all explicitly considered (see Chapter 4 for more detail about this relationship).

The nature of identity in classroom discourse research

All the approaches we have considered in this chapter take a fluid and dynamic view of identity and focus on how identities are (co-)constructed, negotiated and resisted in interaction. How the approaches differ is the scale at which identity is considered. This has resulted in a range of distinctions between different types, roles and levels of identity. It is impossible to focus on all aspects of identity simultaneously, yet each offers a way of studying the ways that classrooms support or constrain the development of students and teachers' identities. Alongside Zimmerman's distinctions between discourse, situated and transportable identities, Gee (2000) identifies four ways in which identity can be viewed by researchers: the nature perspective; the institutional perspective; the discursive perspective and the affinity perspective. Each of these perspectives emphasizes a different aspect of how identities come into being and how are they are sustained in and through interaction. The nature perspective includes identities that relate to biological or natural forces that are outside of our control, such as being white or being a twin. These identities are usually considered at the level of the storyline but if they are made explicit during an interaction then they can also be considered at the interactional level. The institutional perspective considers those identities that are ascribed to us by the institution in which we find ourselves, such as teacher or student. What it means to be a teacher or a student is shaped by the institution of the school and these identities come with specific rights and responsibilities. It is the school that defines what it means to be a teacher (Foucault 1977). This is the perspective usually taken within critical approaches, with a view to challenging these definitions of what it means to be a student or a teacher.

The discursive perspective considers how the discourse of others determines our identity. Identity is characterized by how other people treat us, act towards us, talk about us and interact with us. Both positioning theory and ethnomethodological approaches take this perspective. Finally, the affinity perspective considers identity through the practices in which we engage. The people with whom we share these practices are an 'affinity group'. Again, this perspective considers identity at the level of storyline, but relies more on stories and narratives around identity than the institutional perspective. A classic example includes the work of Brown and colleagues (1993), who focused on what it meant for a classroom to be a 'community of learners'. These classrooms are marked by an emphasis on collaborative learning and other collaborative practices and knowledge is seen as distributed across the members of the classroom, their practices and the tools that they use. These in turn create distinctive identity for learners where they are responsible for each other's learning as well as their own. Here identity is considered with a focus of an affinity group.

Other researchers have offered alternative ways of distinguishing between different forms of identity. Sfard and Prusak (2005) contrast actual and designated identities. Cobb et al. (2009) distinguish between normative and personal identities. In case example 7.3 Anderson identifies the notion of a performative identity and Solomon (2007) describes a participative identity which refers to the ways in which identity is constructed or co-constructed through participation and engagement in a particular group. Identity is also often treated as something that is performative, hence the term performative identity. Holland et al. (1998: 53) talk about 'dramatized worlds' synonymously with figured worlds and many other authors talking about participants enacting particular identities (e.g. Gee 2000). Each of these distinctions serves a purpose in allowing the researcher to contrast different aspects of identities that are consequential for the teachers and students involved, but each distinction also results in particular aspects of the nature of identity, or the process of identity formation or evolution, to be emphasized over others.

Out of the approaches considered so far, there is some consistency in how identity is conceived. Each considers identity to be constructed and developed in interaction. Wenger (1999) describes identity as 'not an object, but a constant becoming' (pp.

153–154) and Holland et al. (1998: 3) also talk about 'identity-making processes'. Identity can also be multiple, multi-faceted and sometimes contradictory. The construction of identity or identities is reflexive and collaborative. Identity is thus treated as a property of the situational context, not the individual participants in the interaction.

How you conceptualize identities will depend on a range of other features of your research, including the context in which it will be taking place. For example, the understanding of the term 'discourse' can also affect how we can approach the analysis of classroom interaction. The distinction Gee (2000) makes between 'discourse' (with a little d) and 'Discourse' (with a capital D) is usually the most significant distinction. 'discourse' usually includes spoken and written words and often includes gestures, eye gaze and other semiotic systems or representations that are used by students and teachers when they interact. 'Discourse' on the other hand includes wider societal meta-narratives, or storylines, within which the interaction is taking place. The nature of identity needs to reflect whether the analysis will focus on 'discourse', 'Discourse' or the interaction between them both.

While each of the approaches treats identity as constructed and negotiated in interaction, there remains the issue of whether identity is also something that it is inside us, a 'core' identity which is a product of our minds and socialization practices. For those using ethnomethodological approaches this is not an issue as it is not relevant to the analysis. They do not even enter into the discussion of whether this 'core' identity exists or its nature and origin if it does.

Another issue is the relationship between people's agency and the macro structures that influence interactions. To what extent are we free to construct our own identities and to what extent is this construction constrained by the social, cultural or political structures we are interacting within. CA and DP again do not engage in this debate, focusing solely on what happens in the interaction itself, yet the other approaches, particularly CDA emphasize the role structures have on influencing the development of identities.

As a researcher you will have your own social and cultural knowledge in relation to the contexts you are researching. A pure ethnomethodological approach asks you to set this knowledge aside and not draw upon it in any analysis. You may know that the teacher is female, but if gender is not oriented to as a category in interaction that it is not relevant to the analysis. Yet there are situations where this local knowledge is what enables you to make sense of the interaction, it is your awareness of the broader social and cultural issues that enables you to see an utterance as orienting to gender as an issue (McAvoy 2016).

Conclusion

This chapter presents an overview of how different theoretical frameworks influence the conceptualization and study of identity in classroom interaction. We encourage you to reflect on your current views around the nature of identity and its role in classrooms and the methodological implications these may have. The key is distinguishing between whether you are interested in identities as something associated with an individual, identities as joint accomplishments negotiated in interaction, or as interactional objects that are used by teachers and students to achieve particular things. Decisions around your research design are driven by these distinctions.

Further reading

Preece, S. (2016), *The Routledge handbook of language and identity*, London: Routledge. This book is a comprehensive guide to a range of approaches to studying the relationship between language and identity, including using the approaches described in this chapter. While not specific to education, it will give you insight into ways in which the methodological approaches have implemented in different ways in the study of identity.

Benwell, B. and E. Stokoe (2006), *Discourse and identity*, Edinburgh: Edinburgh University Press. The first chapter of this book offers a through exploration of the theories surrounding identity and the development of these over time. The rest of the book illustrates a use of these theories in a range of contexts.

CHAPTER EIGHT

Researching Multilingual Classrooms

Introduction

Classrooms are becoming increasingly diverse around the world. Many students are bilingual or multilingual, with students within a single classroom able to communicate in a variety of languages. There are now a range of education policies and practices involving teaching and learning using multiple languages. These include situations where the goal is to spread the use of a nationally recognized language, to spread the use of a language associated with economic competitiveness, or to protect languages from becoming obsolete. With this increase in diversity, into what many describe as a superdiverse society (Vertovec 2007), there has been an increase in the research studies of these classrooms. This in turn has led to conceptualizations and reconceptualizations of language and its role in teaching and learning. In this chapter we examine some of the more recent research and how this has influenced these conceptualizations. We have focused on the role of language in learning particular disciplines, such as mathematics or science, rather than on language learning itself. There is extensive classroom discourse research that focuses on language learning which has been synthesized elsewhere for the interested reader (e.g. Murphy 2014; Farr 2016).

Within educational research there are a range of ways of understanding the role of language in learning. These include language as a complex adaptive system (e.g. Ellis and Larsen-Freeman 2009), ecological perspectives on language learning (e.g. van Lier 2006) or theories of language socialization (e.g. Duff 2007). Common to all the approaches we consider here is the move away from the notion of separate languages as bounded systems of specific words, grammatical structures and other linguistic features (Jørgensen et al. 2011). Instead linguistic features are something we use to communicate in the best way that we can. In the multilingual contexts in which we often find ourselves, languages mutually influence each other, thus making it ideological when we try to separate them. Instead many researchers (e.g. Canagarajah 2013; Barwell 2018) now talk about linguistic repertoires rather than separate languages.

Thus, the unit of analysis has shifted from a focus solely on the language students are using to the variety of ways in linguistic features can be associated with particular social or cultural contexts (Blommaert and Rampton 2011). As Blommaert (2016: 247) argues, 'established terms, such as "code-switching" and even "multilingualism" exhaust the limits of their descriptive and explanatory adequacy in the face of such highly complex blends' of linguistic and communicative resources. Local knowledge then becomes crucial when we try to make sense of how teachers and students are using linguistic features or when we try to understand how students and teachers see themselves in relation to the repertoires they use (Makoni and Pennycook 2012).

Teachers and students can draw upon their own languages in interaction for a variety of purposes, pedagogical and social: content development, language development, and sociocultural integration (Pontier and Gort 2016). Spotti and Blommaert sum this shift up nicely when they say:

A sociolinguistic perspective rooted in the study of language and superdiversity therefore looks at people and at their communicative repertoires neither as something that is owned nor as something that can be used purely for a communicative purpose – that is, rather than looking at language as a noun, the perspective [is of] language as a verb, as something that people do. (Spotti and Blommaert 2016: 171)

Research in multilingual contexts can draw on a range of fields, each of which has its preferred theoretical approaches, conceptualizations of the role of language and methodologies. These include bilingual education, applied linguistics, second language acquisition, language teaching, linguistics, English as a Foreign/ Additional language, TESOL, English for Academic Purposes and English as the Medium of Instruction. There are also a range of educational contexts in which research involving multilingual learners can take place with bilingual, monolingual, immersion classrooms to name just a few.

With this diverse range of fields comes a proliferation of terminology. There are also debates and disagreements both between and within these fields, as well as a blurring of the boundaries between them. In this chapter we will touch on only a few of these debates but we invite you to consider the conceptualizations of language and the role of language within these debates and how these might influence the design of research.

Case example 8.1:

Language brokering in a middle school science class (Bayley et al. 2005)

Context: In many classrooms across the world, classes include students who are fairly new to the language of instruction and whose home language is not spoken by their teacher, but is shared with other students in the class. This study describes one classroom where a newly arrived Spanish-speaking student was learning science through the medium of English in a US classroom. In common with many new immigrant students, this student did not understand enough English to understand the classroom interactions in which he was expected to participate. In this study the teacher was an English monolingual while the majority of students were of Mexican descent; these students had a range of levels of English proficiency ranging from absolute beginner to intermediate. There were approximately an equal number of bilingual and monolingual English and Spanish speakers.

Goal: Language brokering is used to describe the informal translation that peers offer to support someone who does not sufficiently understand the language of instruction to be able to make sense of the interactions taking place. The goal of the analysis was to examine what types of information are made available to the struggling student through this informal translation or language brokering. Specifically, what types of teacher talk were being translated, and what types were not being translated.

Outcomes: The analysis shows that procedural instructions were more frequently translated compared to teacher talk about concepts. For example, on occasions the teacher would invite the students to translate the procedures they would need to carry out. Similarly, some of the Spanish monolingual students would ask for translations but these were often responded to with translations of the instructions of what to do, rather than translations of what the teacher had just said. Bayley, Hansen-Thomas and Langman argue that this may be because these instructions generally used relatively familiar language, in contrast to the scientific explanations of new academic content by the teacher.

Research methods: Science lessons for one seventh-grade class were audio and video recorded for a full school year. The students mostly worked in groups and three of these groups were recorded and two researchers also took field notes. All the audio and video recordings were transcribed orthographically. The research team also collected documentation about the English proficiency of those students involved as it became available during the year. Teacher turns were then coded as to whether they were concerned with class management, behaviour management, an announcement, procedural knowledge, or declarative knowledge. In the paper the examples focus on one particular student, Manuel, who had never studied English before being placed in all-English classes in the school.

Language as a tool or a resource

As a way of challenging the deficit view that prevailed in research looking at the learning of language learners, many researchers draw upon the sociocultural idea of language as a tool, or a resource that students can use to benefit their learning. Language is therefore 'a resource to be managed, developed and conserved' (Ruiz 1984: 28).

However, language is not a neutral 'resource'. Whenever teachers or students use a particular word or phrase, the meaning of this word or phrase is associated with the other people who have used this word previously. Ricento (2005), for example, argues that the idea of language as a resource supports existing language ideologies rather than challenging them. This is evident in several studies where language is treated as a tool or a resource with which to learn English or mathematics (e.g. Planas and Setati 2009). Barwell (2018) argues that research that uses the idea of language as a resource separates out its role in teaching and learning from 'broader social aspects of language use, such as in constructing identities, reproducing social norms and structures, or maintaining various ideological positions about languages and learners' (p. 159).

A lot of the research focusing on language as a resource uses the idea of code-switching, where students switch between their two (or more) languages, and in classrooms this often means using their home language when drawing on their everyday experiences and the language of instruction for technical vocabulary (Karlsson 2015). This practice of code-switching has led to arguments for allowing students to use their home languages in the classroom to support their learning. This use of code-switching between languages has also led to different ways of researchers conceptualizing the use of different languages in the classroom including translanguaging and communicative repertoires which we discuss next.

One example of code-switching by teachers comes from the work of Setati and colleagues working in the South African context. For example, Setati and Adler (2000) investigated how teachers' language choices affected students' learning of mathematics. Their analysis detailed the tensions teachers felt as they balanced their use of English as the language of instruction and the need to use the native languages of their students to support their learning of mathematics. Teachers in the rural schools particularly felt the pressure to use English, as their students were less likely to encounter English outside of school. Setati and Adler documented numerous situations where teachers code-switched into their students' native languages. This code-switching served a range of purposes:

> On the one hand as teachers they needed to switch languages in order to reformulate a question or instruction, or to reexplain a concept, and they needed to encourage their learners to use their main language in order to facilitate communication and understanding. At the same time however, it was their responsibility to induct their learners into mathematical English and hence it was important to use English in the mathematics classroom as much as possible. (p. 255)

Translanguaging

Translanguaging describes how bilingual and multilingual speakers flexibly use a variety of linguistic resources as they make sense of their worlds (Garcia and Wei 2014), but also refers to a pedagogy for teaching and learning. Baker (2011: 288) defined translanguaging as the process of 'making meaning, shaping experiences, gaining understanding and knowledge through the use of two languages'. García argues that bilingual students translanguage in order to construct meaning in the classroom. Her conceptualization of translanguaging includes the idea of transformation, where translanguaging has the potential to challenge contexts where there one language has hegemony. Garcia treats translanguaging as a 'new way of being, acting and languaging in a different social, cultural, and political context, allowing fluid discourses to flow, and giving voice to new social realities' (Blackledge and Creese 2014: 11). Furthermore, García and Wei (2014) argue that translanguaging is different from code-switching in that it does not simply describe a shift between two languages, but to the creation and use of original and complex interrelated discursive practices. Some researchers argue that there is no separation of languages in the mind of the multilingual person. From an analytic perspective, translanguaging is often considered to be an observable behaviour of a participant that can be the focus of research.

More people in the world are now bilingual rather than monolingual and many would argue that it is consequently very important that bilingualism is normalized in the classroom too (Murphy 2014). A translanguaging approach to teaching and learning normalizes bilingualism, in that it aims to enable students to draw on all their linguistic resources in order to maximize their understanding and attainment. In a similar way to the code-switching research this approach advocates for students being able to draw on all their languages in their learning. The shift to a focus on translanguaging has also led to an increase of research looking at the identity and agency of students as they use, create and interpret linguistic resources when they communicate in classrooms. Studies making use of the idea of translanguaging consider the language practices of all the students within a class 'in order to develop new language practices and sustain old ones, communicate and appropriate knowledge, and give voice to new socio-political realities by interrogating linguistic inequality' (García and Kano 2014: 61). One such study is that of Pontier and Gort (2016) and is described in case example 8.2. They look at translanguaging in pedagogy and how this affects the language development of their students.

Case example 8.2:

Coordinated translanguaging pedagogy as distributed cognition: a case study of two dual language bilingual education preschool co-teachers' languaging practices during shared book readings (Pontier and Gort 2016)

Context: This study is situated within the context of dual language bilingual education and makes use of the idea of distributed cognition (Hutchins 1995) to describe the coordination of instructional goals and translanguaging practices.

Goal: To identify the ways in which teachers' bilingualism was a resource within different practices and to achieve different instructional goals.

Outcome: The analysis illustrates how teachers draw upon their own bilingualism and their co-teacher's bilingualism to engage in flexible language performances that sometimes reflected the monolingual languaging norms, and at other times reflected bilingual languaging norms. They show how this translanguaging supports the language and literacy development of their bilingual students.

Research methods: This ethnographic study took place in a Spanish–English dual language bilingual education preschool in the United States. In this preschool each classroom has two teachers, one as a model for English and one as a model for Spanish, though both of the teachers and also the students are bilingual. There were seventeen students in the class aged three to four years. Daily shared book-readings were video-recorded and field notes were taken by three researchers acting as non-participant observers. The language of the shared book-readings switched on a weekly basis between Spanish and English. This activity lasted around fifteen minutes and the analysis was performed on a total of six hours of video recordings that included both the usual class teachers. Those parts of the video that involved both teachers and were focused on academic activities were transcribed and the transcriptions included details of gestures and other semiotic resources.

The researchers used distributed cognition to frame the analysis of the simultaneous interactions between two teachers and their students. This is combined with the translanguaging perspective focusing on languages as practices that the teachers use. The first level of analysis examined the language instructional strategies the teachers utilized. The second level recorded the languages the teachers used, whether they spoke solely in English, solely in Spanish or moved between the two. The researchers then used a constant comparative analysis (Glaser and Strauss 1967).

It should be said, however, that the distinction between code-switching and translanguaging is not as clear cut as some of the literature presents it to be (Park 2012). This is largely due to the different ways in which code-switching is treated within the literature, and its focus on identifying the languages involved and the structural or functional role that the change in language plays. In contrast, translanguaging research tends to emphasize the processes of sense-making in which the different languages are used. The questions are around how linguistic resources are used to make meaning, rather than what resources are used when. The origins of code-switching and translanguaging may also explain the difficulties in distinguishing between the two. Code-switch is a linguistic concept with a long history of use in research, whereas translanguaging was initially developed as a pedagogy that deliberately made use of two languages to help students make sense of ideas (Baker and Sienkewicz 2000). Both translanguaging and code-switching refer to students changing between languages in a fluid and natural way, and both advocate for students being able to use all of their languages in the classroom.

Language as political

A great deal of research into multilingual classrooms has focused on classrooms where English is the Medium of Instruction or on students who are English learners within bilingual or multilingual classrooms. This in itself is a bias within the field of education that is only recently being challenged. Many studies of bilingual classrooms with a range of approaches to supporting and developing both languages still show that English is emphasized over the other language despite policies and the language preferences of the teachers (Enyedy et al. 2008; Flores 2016; Reyes 2004). Other studies have shown that bilingual students switch between their languages depending upon the complexity of what they are trying to do (Planas and Setati 2009). More recently there has been a rise in the number of studies that have emphasized the benefits of bilingualism. One example, where the focus is also on Spanish learners, is given in case example 8.3.

Case example 8.3:

Becoming 'spanish learners': Identity and interaction among multilingual children in a Spanish–English dual language classroom (Martínez et al. 2017)

Context: A longitudinal qualitative study of language and ideology at one public school in southern California. The study focused on a cohort of bi- and multilingual students and their teachers beginning when they entered the school in the kindergarten/first-grade classroom and followed them through the year groups as they progressed over several years. The study focused on a Spanish–English dual language strand within the school, and the students came from a working-class immigrant community, with the majority of the students being Latino/a. There were no white children in the school. This study was ethnographic and collected data through participant observation, video recordings of lessons, samples of students' work and semi-structured interviews with both the students and the teachers.

Goal: To identify what identities were co-constructed by and for two particular students, Alicia and Malik, as they learned Spanish, and to examine how these identities were co-constructed within the context of everyday classroom interactions. Importantly the goal is not to show *that* these identities were constructed and contested, but rather *how* they were constructed and contested at the interactional level.

Outcome: The analysis illustrates how different students position themselves and are positioned by each other as expert Spanish speakers, expert bilingual speakers as well as competent learners. These identity claims are made by speaking in either English or Spanish at different points of the interaction as well as by translanguaging. They are also contested through the correction of lexical errors. The authors argue that it is the combining of English and Spanish that enables the students to position themselves as bilingual. The two Spanish-learning students who were the focus in the analysis were treated differently in the interaction. Alicia spoke entirely in English, but demonstrated her understanding of Spanish in the ways that she responded to what the other students said. Malik on the other hand used a mixture of Spanish and English, but his language and the content of his turns were corrected by others. Within the wider study, despite similarities in the accuracy of the Spanish spoken by both Alicia and Malik, Alicia was mostly positioned as a competent Spanish speaker, while Malik was mostly positioned as a less than competent Spanish speaker.

Research methods: The analysis in the paper is based on a single interaction between the teacher and four students in the Kindergarten/first-grade classroom. These four students had different language and cultural backgrounds. Alicia's parents immigrated from the Philippines and she was fluent in English and spoke Tagalog and English at home. Malik came from a Sudanese background and was also fluent in English but spoke mostly Arabic at home, and some English with his sister. Karla was fluent in both English and Spanish and spoke both at home, she was equally comfortable in both languages and was considered to be a proficient bilingual. Javier was born in Mexico and spoke Spanish at home but had limited English proficiency. The focus of the paper was on Alicia and Malik who were both learning Spanish and the authors identified how they formed identities as Spanish speakers or learners as they interacted with their Spanish-speaking classmates and teacher. To analyse the short interaction they used Erickson's (2004) ethnographic microanalysis of social interaction. This is an approach based on ethnomethodology and CA but sits within wider ethnographic studies and draws heavily on positioning theory when analysing identity work.

Case example 8.3 illustrates a focus on the identities of bilingual students within a dual language classroom. The concept of identity is prevalent in research that looks at the politics of language policy and practices around the world. Planas (2011), for example, looks at identity in bilingual classrooms in Catalonia where both Spanish and Catalan are official languages, but some students are Catalan dominant and others are Spanish dominant. Multilingual classrooms reflect a range of social and cultural discourse and ideologies and identity research within this context often focuses on how students' and teachers' identities are affected by the language hierarchies within the classroom.

Researchers who are interested in the ideologies, hegemony or endorsement of language in practice draw substantially from

CDA (see Chapter 4) and his approach which aims to reveal the connections between language, power and ideology (Fairclough 1989). Martínez-Roldán and Malavé (2004), for example, examined the role of language ideology in the development of bilingual students' literacy and in their identities as bilingual students, some of which undermined the goals of the bilingual education they were receiving, and some of which supported it.

The socio-political view of language in relation to multilingual classrooms draws heavily from Cummins's (2000, 2016) work, who argues for the power of researchers and educators to address issues of equity, and Myers-Scotton (2006), who considered language and interaction as a negotiation of rights and obligations. Cummins's threshold theory, where learners with a certain level of language proficiency can transfer knowledge between languages through a common underlying proficiency (CUP), is frequently cited in arguments advocating for both bilingual education and monolingual classrooms.

In research, this issue of language as political also raises issues around how we label the teachers and students we are researching. To date, most research describes students as English learners but this label reifies a category focused narrowly on what these students do not yet know. This label also perpetuates the deficit view of students rather than acknowledging the heterogeneity within students labelled this way.

Another way in which the political aspects of language choice is brought to the fore is in the rise of English as Medium of Instruction in countries where English is neither an official language nor a majority language (e.g. Wächter and Maiworm 2008). Here university courses, particularly in science, technology and engineering, are taught through the medium of English with the aim of enabling the students to engage with literature published in English, but also to improve graduate employability and international recognitions of the university institution itself.

Communicative repertoires

Another theoretical idea that researchers, particular those using sociolinguistics (see Chapter 5), draw upon when studying multilingual classrooms is that of communicative repertoires (Rymes

2015). Communicative repertoires are the collection of ways people use language and other forms of communication, such as gestures, the way they dress, or the way they behave, to function effectively in the multiple communities and contexts in which they participate. This idea of repertoires within linguistics developed out of Gumperz's (1964) notion of a verbal repertoire, which brought together ideas around mixing languages and the social effects of linguistic choices. Researchers drawing on other theories, such as the work of Bakhtin, also use the term communicative repertoires in a similar way (e.g. Barwell 2018; Alexander 2018). Communicative repertoires have a broader meaning than translanguaging in that while someone's communicative repertoire may include several languages, it could also just consist of a range of varieties within one language. Language is just one element of a communicative repertoire. Rymes (2015) argues that focusing on communicative repertoires in the classroom shifts attention away from the 'correctness' of the language to how students and teachers use and negotiate different repertoires as they interact.

To use the idea of communicative repertoires in research we need to be able to distinguish between different repertoires. This is complex as these distinctions can include the use of particular words, ways of communicating, gestures and interactional structures. Yet, it is these additional distinctions that do not focus solely on language choice that make the idea of communicative repertoires different from the other ideas offered in this chapter. The term repertoire is also used more widely to describe the diversity in forms of knowledge that students bring with them into the classroom. Research using the notion of communicative repertoires largely focuses on the differences between the repertoires students use outside the classroom and those they use inside the classroom (see Martinez et al. 2017 for a review of this research).

Conclusion

Research involving multilingual classrooms is diverse in terms of its focus, its theoretical perspectives, its terminology and its aims. We have explored just a few ideas drawn on by researchers specifically interested in classroom discourse which focus on the variations in how language is acting or being used within the classroom. Language as a resource and translanguaging-focused research generally focuses on how language is used, whereas language as political focuses more on the social and cultural impact of language and language use on teachers and students. Communicative repertoires also consider the social and cultural role of language in teaching and learning by considering the 'traces of past times and present times, of live lived locally and globally' (Creese and Blackledge 2011: 1206).

Researching multilingual classrooms brings with it additional challenges in that as a researcher you need to be familiar with the languages or even the communicative repertoires being used in order to make sense of them and how they may be influencing the focus of your research. However, in some classrooms the sheer diversity of languages and cultures within the class means this is not possible. While some of the approaches discussed in this chapter will still enable you to examine when particular languages are used and in what contexts they are being used, addressing the issues of how and why they are being used requires you as a researcher to be familiar with both the language and the social and cultural implications associated with that language used. While these can be partially studied through interviews and using the perspectives of the learners themselves, this is not always possible or appropriate, for example with very young children. If you want to research multilingual classrooms then you may want to discuss with your peers and others with experience of research in this context both your focus of research and any methods you propose to use.

Further Reading

Cummins, J. and M. Swain (1986), *Bilingualism in education: Aspects of theory, research and practice*, Abingdon, OX: Routledge. This book offers a synthesis of both theoretical and empirical research of the time drawing on a range of approaches in relation to the education of bilingual students.

The special issue of *Language and education* (2013) 27 (4) on multilingual resources in classroom interaction: ethnographic and discourse analytic perspectives consider a range of approaches to studying classroom discourse in multilingual classrooms as well as a range of contexts. For an overview of this special issue read the introductory article by Saxena and Martin-Jones (2013).

CHAPTER NINE

Knowledge and Knowing

Introduction

In this chapter we will explore how studying knowledge and understanding by examining classroom discourse affects how we conceptualize knowledge or knowing, how we distinguish between different types of knowledge and also the different foci researchers have taken to studying knowledge or types of knowledge within interaction.

In classrooms, and in classroom research, a key focus has been on the acquisition or transfer of knowledge, but classrooms are also a place where students (and teachers) demonstrate what they know and use knowledge to achieve particular things. Traditionally, knowledge has largely been investigated through testing students, or in-depth interviews exploring their knowledge and understanding of particular topics. Such studies have also generally focused on what students (or teachers) do not know or do not understand. In contrast, as we will explore below, studies of classroom interaction tend to focus on the diversity of ways in which students understand ideas, and how they draw on different sources of knowledge, including shared knowledge, as they interact in classrooms. Learning is about doing knowing or being knowledgeable rather than having knowledge, and studies of classroom interaction focus on the construction, re-construction, negotiation and sharing of knowledge.

The way in which classroom interaction supports or hinders the development of knowledge is an area of considerable debate (Schwarz et al. 2009). Much research into classroom interaction and its relationship to knowledge and learning has focused on questioning. In classrooms questions are normally asked to find out what students know, rather than because the teacher asking the question does not know, as would be the case when someone asked a question in 'real life'. This focus on questioning includes the now well-known and debated identification of the Initiation–Response–Evaluation (IRE) (Mehan 1979; Sinclair and Coulthard 1975) sequence that dominates most pedagogical interactions. Different researchers approach the use of the IRE structure in contrasting ways. Alexander (2018) and Mercer (2002) treat the IRE as something to be avoided or limited in classroom interaction and often equate this structure with short closed questions that require students to do little more than recall knowledge. Other researchers (e.g. Wells 1993) take a broader view, focusing on the structure as a pattern of turn-taking rather than its function. From a CA perspective, open questions and extended student responses also usually have the IRE structure. The focus of research is then what teachers and students do with their turns within this structure (e.g. Lee 2008). This structure is what enables the teacher to react and respond to what students have said and to manage the direction of discussions. It is also how teachers can evaluate or connect students' claims, responses or contributions to the accepted knowledge of the wider community, be that the knowledge represented in the textbook, the knowledge generally accepted within the discipline or the knowledge generally accepted within classrooms (Kim and Roth 2018).

Classrooms are generally considered as having a teacher who is knowledgeable and students who are there to learn from this teacher. That is, teachers and students have asymmetrical epistemic statuses (Heller 2017). This asymmetry also means that it is usually students who make mistakes or do not know something they need during a task, and it is usually the teacher who corrects or points out these errors or gives students the knowledge they need to continue. Studies of classroom discourse are interested in how this learning or transfer of knowledge takes place through classroom interactions or engagement with curriculum materials.

The nature of knowledge

Everyone who is interested in the development of knowledge makes assumptions about the nature of knowledge itself. Some focus on the individual and their interactions with the world, including other people (e.g. Atwood et al. 2010; Chapman 2009). Here knowledge is something that belongs to the individual and knowledge is acquired from others sharing (or transmitting) their knowledge. Learning involves the individual internalizing this knowledge. Others focus on the group of people interacting and how the shared knowledge of the group is developed (e.g. case example 9.2, Pontier and Gort [2016]). Here 'the knowledge' does not reside in one single individual, or in each of the members of the group, but rather is distributed between them. This is the main premise of distributed cognition (e.g. Brown et al. 1993; Pontier and Gort 2016). Others still focus on the interaction itself (e.g. Heritage 2012a; Koole 2012), where knowledge or knowing is treated as an interactional object to be acted upon or with by different people.

When the focus of research is on classroom discourse, interest shifts from what knowledge individuals have, to how issues around knowledge, knowing or understanding are handled in interaction or in texts. This interest can vary from examining how shared knowledge is established (e.g. Edwards and Mercer 1987), to how teachers and students position themselves as knowledgeable or not (e.g. Barwell 2013), or the ways in which teachers and/or authors use texts to reinforce or challenge social or cultural norms around or interpretations of 'knowledge' (e.g. case example 9.5; Schall-Leckrone and Barron 2018).

This raises the questions of what does it mean to know something? Who is it that knows? What is it that is known? How did they come to know? How can we answer these questions through the analysis of classroom discourse? For example, at a very simple level students being able to repeat definitions or phrases in interaction may or may not indicate that a student has learnt something or that they have understood that thing. Some would argue that knowledge only truly exists when it is used and applied, for example through the claims and evidence students draw on in their arguments (Kim and Roth 2018). Others argue that knowledge is more than just a collection of facts, but includes ways of behaving and arguing that are context-specific, developing habits of mind (e.g. Cuoco et al. 1996; Erduran et al. 2004). Thus knowing mathematics, for example, means knowing how to approach problems in a mathematical way, or appreciating the nature of proof that is specific to mathematics.

Discourse approaches to the consideration of knowledge or knowing treat knowledge as relative to a particular community, so what is knowledge for one community, may not be for another (van Dijk 2012). Knowledge is also contextual, in that what counts as knowledge in one classroom may not count in everyday life or in another classroom, for example. This feature of knowledge is used by teachers and students when they interact. Certain knowledge can be treated as assumed and does not need to be stated if it is likely to be known by everyone in the classroom. Chevallard (1991) used the metaphor of life to describe knowledge: knowledge 'lives' within groups of people which emphasizes the context-boundedness of knowledge. This idea has been used to distinguish between 'knowledge to be taught' which comes from textbooks and the curriculum, and the 'taught knowledge' which is specific to the classroom in which it was 'taught' (Tiberghien and Malkoun 2009).

The first case example in this chapter illustrates one of the most common ways that knowledge is considered in classroom interaction research. Here knowledge is viewed as co-constructed by teachers and students and shows how the nature of this co-construction changes over time.

Case example 9.1:

The construction of knowledge in classroom talk (Atwood et al. 2010)

Context: This study takes an individualistic stance on the nature of knowledge. The study focused on audio recordings of university psychology classes, on the basis that in psychology classes knowledge is negotiated rather than treated as a matter of established facts. While the study uses the techniques of CA, it is situated within a sociocultural framework rather than having its basis in ethnomethodology. The seating arrangements, goals and beliefs of the teachers, teaching resources used are all considered in the analysis.

Goal: To detail the micro-level structures of classroom talk through which knowledge was co-constructed by teachers and students.

Outcomes: The nature of classroom talk developed from mostly disputational or cumulative talk in first-year classes, to exploratory talk in fourth-year classes.

Methods: Two classes of first-year college and two classes of fourth-year university psychology course were the focus of the particular analysis in this paper, a first-year class where the students were sitting in rows, and a fourth-year class where students were seated in a circle. The interactions of the groups were recorded, transcribed and then analysed using a CA and social pragmatic approach (Turnbull 2003). The analysis began using a CA approach to identify and describe the structures of interaction that related to learning. This includes analysing turn-taking, adjacency pairs and repair. The second stage of analysis then focused on connecting these structures to Mercer's exploratory, disputational or cumulative talk and Piaget's (1932/1965, 1977/1995) notions of cooperation and constraint. Exploratory talk is marked by joint reasoning where the methods for reasoning are explicit in interaction. Cumulative talk involves building a shared understanding but without any critique or challenging of claims. Disputational talk is competitive and is marked by students being unwilling to take into account the perspectives of the other students and sticking to their own argument (Mercer 2000).

Ethnomethodological approaches view learning and displays of knowing as embedded in everyday social life. Those who use such approaches are interested in how knowledge is co-produced in interaction or in how knowledge is treated as an interactional object. Within CA, the ideas of *epistemic status* and *epistemic stance* (Heritage 2012a, b, 2013) are widely used to distinguish between types of knowledge and who has rights to know within interactions. Epistemic status refers to the idea that when two people interact, one participant will be treated as more knowledgeable or less knowledgeable than the other (Heritage 2013). The focus of the analysis is then on the ways in which the epistemic status of participants is made observable in interactions, and how this changes during the interaction. This moment-by-moment change involves claims of knowledge, or claims of insufficient knowledge, but also marking knowledge as reliable, certain or inferred. Epistemic stance refers to the observable actions participants use in these moment-by-moment changes. To some extent, the institutional categories of teacher and student determine epistemic statuses, in that in relation to the content of a lesson the teacher is usually the more knowledgeable participant. In contrast to everyday interactions, these institutionally bound differences in epistemic statuses are 'transparent' (Stivers et al. 2011). However, this epistemic authority can be challenged and contested in interaction (Kääntä 2014).

One way in which the institutionally inferred epistemic statuses are 'transparent' or observable is through the IRE (Mehan 1979) sequences that commonly occur in classrooms. The evaluation turn in particular illustrates the teacher's more knowledgeable status, as this is where they assess or correct their students' responses. The nature of question–answer pairings within this structure is another observable feature of the teacher's more knowledgeable epistemic status in that the questions are not requests for information or knowledge because the teacher does not know the answer, but rather invitations for students to display what they know (Macbeth 2011).

Case example 8.2 takes this CA perspective and focus on epistemic status and epistemic stance to show how students avoid contesting the teacher's epistemic status of being more knowledgeable by how they design their turns when they correct something the teacher has written and treated as correct. This example also makes use of the CA tool of repair outlined in Chapter 2. Both case examples 8.2 and 2.3 illustrate the CA and DP stance of treating knowledge as an interactional object. Both examples illustrate that teachers and students orient to the institutional differences in epistemic authority between teachers and students.

Case example 9.2:

From noticing to initiating correction: Students' epistemic displays in instructional interaction (Käänta 2014)

Context: The study involved developing a classroom data corpus from a range of classrooms in Finland. The corpus included Content-and-Language-Integrated-Learning (CLIL) lessons (in biology, physics, English and history) as well as 12 EFL lessons. The paper focuses on the data from a CLIL English language classroom with fourteen-year-old students.

Goal: To identify and classify the different types of student-initiated repairs or corrections.

Outcomes: The initiation of a correction reveals that the student has the knowledge to notice that there is an error, but at the same time this initiation challenges the teacher's epistemic authority as she has presented the error as correct. However, students orient to this challenge when they initiate the correction by showing a preference for teacher self-correction and giving the teacher space and time to self-correct, both before the initiation and after. The students display their epistemic positions through both their embodied actions such as eye gaze and facial expressions and subsequently through the way that they initiate the correction verbally.

Methods: The researcher combines CA and the analysis of embodiment-in-interaction. The analysis focused on when students initiated a correction on something their teacher had written that was displayed to the class. Analysis includes students' eye gaze shifts and facial expressions and focus on the sequence of an embodied noticing by a student followed by the initiation of a correction.

One way in which issues around knowledge or knowing become observable in classroom discourse is where they challenge the norms. For example, case example 8.2 examines what happens when the epistemic authority is reversed by students initiating a correction on what the teacher has written on the board. Brooks (2016) also uses a focus on corrections and CDA to examine shifts in authority in classroom interaction which disrupt the usual patterns of teacher and student interactions when students share 'personal sides of themselves' when responding to their teacher's questions.

Sociolinguistic approaches to studying knowledge focus on knowledge as a social construction.

Case example 9.3:

Thirty-one is a lot! Assessing four-year-old children's number knowledge during an open-ended activity (Pollitt et al. 2015)

Context: This study is situated within a context of considerable change in early childhood education in Australia, which include debates around the role of play-based curriculums and a shifting emphasis on the role of assessment.

Goal: To explore the diverse ways children demonstrated their number knowledge 'while they traced around wooden numerals, drawing and discussing values of quantity' (p. 13). This was partly in order to develop assessment strategies that both give children the opportunities to demonstrate their knowledge and could be used to gain insight into children's mathematical thinking.

Outcomes: The analysis focused on the mathematical focus of the children's talk and revealed the diversity of ways that the children drew on their knowledge when completing the task, revealing the 'children's dynamic and interrelated understanding of mathematical concepts and highlighting both the range of ideas children bring to mathematical thinking, and children's creative capacity for expressing their mathematical reasoning' (p. 16). The narrative analysis enabled the researchers to reveal that the depth of mathematical knowledge held by a child is not always easily reflected by their knowledge of numerals alone.

Methods: The participants were forty-seven children from three early childhood centres in Melbourne, Australia. Over a period of three weeks the children were given wooden numerals and a range of drawing materials and were invited to draw and discuss their drawing together in small groups along with one of the researchers. The researchers used six prompts during their interactions with the children to encourage them to talk about their work. The study took a narrative inquiry approach to analyse four-year-old children's descriptions of what they are doing and why they are doing it as they trace around wooden numerals. The analysis considered what they said, their gestures, use of concrete objects and what they drew as they took part in the activity. This narrative analysis provided an in-depth approach that enabled the researchers to explore the children's knowledge in greater depth.

Argumentation, interpretation, claims and evidence

Argumentation is a topic that is often the focus of mathematics and science education research (e.g. Erduran 2018; Forman et al. 1998; Krummheuer 2000) and within these disciplines focuses on the reasoning associated with claims and evidence. Interpretation on the other hand is often the focus of textual analysis in English and history classrooms (Chapman 2009; Giovanelli 2017) and the reasoning associated with claims and evidence within the context of these texts. Within classroom discourse research both argumentation and interpretation are considered to be forms of discourse, which vary in their form and structure between disciplines, and consequently they are something that students need support with in using both in written texts and in interaction.

Case example 9.4:

Dialogical argumentation in elementary science classrooms (Kim and Roth 2018)

Context: This study draws on the social–psychological theory of Vygotsky and considers argumentation to be a social relation between teachers and students, in that students may take different parts of the argumentation process, such as making a claim, challenging a claim or providing evidence to support a claim and that it is the interaction and contributions of others that collectively has an argument structure (Kim and Roth 2014). The authors also draw upon a ethnomethodological perspective in that a student's claim is only a claim when they have stated it and another has responded to it, that is, another student or the teacher has treated it as a claim. They consequently define argumentation not as 'the individual components of argumentation structure, such as claim, evidence, warrant, etc. but the dynamic relations of those components emerging from classroom talk' (p. 8). This is reinforced through the use of the CA notion of an adjacency pair as the unit of analysis.

Goal: To investigate the social relations in young children's argumentation in science topics.

Outcomes: The researchers illustrate how the parts of an argument are mostly spread across different speakers, rather being part of an individual's argument. This shows that argumentative patterns exist as social relations. They argue that participation in these social relations of reasoning and argumentation can lead to the development of young children's argumentation.

The researchers also consider the role of the teacher in this process, offering an example of a situation where the teacher challenged a claim but this challenge and the evidence used to support this challenge were not enough to persuade the students that their claim was wrong. This illustrates how the teacher is subject to the same claim-evidence and burden of proof procedures as the students. Thus they argue that argument patterns can be supported by teachers before they are explicitly taught by offering the shift of the burden of proof to the students so that they are encouraged to provide evidence to support claims being made (by them or by others).

Methods: The researchers use a descriptive case study based on one classroom. The data collected was naturally occurring in that there were no interventions around argumentation in this classroom. The students were seven to eight years old in a multi-age classroom in western Canada and the science teacher had more than five years' experience teaching science at this level. The lessons were video recorded using two cameras and both whole-class interactions and small group work of two groups were recorded. These video recordings were then transcribed for analysis. The researchers used *interaction analysis* (Jordan and Henderson 2009), which involves the joint viewing of the videos, stopping whenever one of the researchers has something to say or wants to replay something. All claims and hypotheses from this process are noted and subsequently tested against the remaining data. The analysis focused on the claim and evidence that were made during interactions and how the burden of proof (Walton 1988) shifts in interaction. A burden of proof is where there is an obligation to support a claim made with evidence in order to persuade others.

Aligned with ideas about the nature of claims to knowledge are the statements 'I know', 'I don't know' and 'I don't understand'. 'I don't know' can be a statement of fact, but it can also be a disclaimer from certainty, or a statement of lack of desire to answer a question. The use of these phrases in the classroom could form an interesting study of classroom discourse.

Schema theory

Schema is a term drawn from the field of psychology (originally from the work of Piaget) used to describe a framework or categorization which people use to organize ideas and knowledge that they already have, and into which they fit new ideas and knowledge as they encounter them. Existing schemata enable us to process new information quickly, allowing us to cope with rapidly changing knowledge environments (such as a lesson!). They can also colour the ways in which we understand and process new information; existing perceptions can prevent us from accepting new information, or cause us to miscategorize it. A stereotype is an example of a schema which might cause problems in processing. In the classroom environment, if a student who is normally disruptive and makes tenuous points in order to divert the class suddenly makes an extremely perceptive and thoughtful point, which is a genuine challenge to what the teacher has been saying, existing schematic representations of that student may prevent others from accepting the basis of that challenge. Case example 10.1 draws on schema theory, in that pre-existing representations of a novel mean that new knowledge about it can only be constructed in certain, pre-directed ways. Case example 9.5 suggests how the construction of certain schemata in school can influence later understanding of broader topics.

Schema theory is particularly relevant to educational research in the teaching of reading (Rumelhart 2017) and literature (Giovanelli 2016). When we read, we develop a schema of the particular text, but it also exists within a wider schema of how stories operate. It is this that enables the twist ending to a short story to be so satisfying: it surprises us because our schema did not predict it. In literacy and literature education research schema theory is often linked with understanding of genre and generic expectations.

Schema theory is related to some of the ways in which Vygotsky characterizes learning, but in contrast it has an emphasis on the ways in which individuals encounter and organize knowledge. As well as being an interesting approach to learning in the classroom, it can be a fruitful lens for looking at the ways in which teachers develop knowledge of individuals and groups within their classrooms and schools.

What counts as knowledge: A critical view

'Powerful knowledge' is a concept that draws on the work of sociologist Emile Durkheim to suggest that specialized and differentiated knowledge (i.e. academic knowledge) is more advantageous to the holder than other types of knowledge and that this has implications for what we should include in curricula (Young and Muller 2013). As Young and Muller argue, we as humans make a distinction between knowledge and our opinions and experience, making a claim that knowledge is of a 'real' world, distinct from us. Recently debates in the United States, England and Australia have all considered what constitutes powerful knowledge, in particular drawing on the concept of cultural literacy (Hirsch 1987), in the context of debates about social justice and reducing the educational advantage of those with higher socio-economic status. By focusing on the potential for knowledge to emancipate the holder and enable social mobility via educational success, the debates have hidden an important factor, which is that 'knowledge' is often contested and that even where it is not contested, the elements which are chosen for teaching can often obscure the whole truth. Textbooks cannot include all knowledge on a given topic, and are written by people with specific views for a specific purpose. In other areas exhortations to 'teach the controversy!' may obscure where there is a generally agreed consensus on the facts of the case, a move which is 'pedagogically irresponsible' (Scott and Branch 2003: 499).

Whitty, in a well-known foundational text in this area, argues that given the constructed nature of curricula and textbooks (a construction which often happens under little scrutiny) 'pupils were likely to accept as immutable "fact" what was but one ideological version of the world' (1985: 19). This has been a focus of considerable critical research in recent years as researchers challenge the ways in which 'knowledge' is socially constructed and portrayed to consumers (i.e. teachers and pupils). Case example 4.3 (Sharma and Buxton 2015) is one example, using the case of science textbooks. Case example 9.5 is another, in which history textbooks are the subject of a critical analysis of their portrayal of the Abolition Movement. History texts are particularly fruitful areas of investigation in relation to the social construction of knowledge, in that they are 'not likely to straightforwardly, unproblematically relate the "facts" of history, just as they are' (Barnard 2003). Indeed, history teaching and learning is often part of nation-building efforts, which are designed to shape citizens' national identities (Carretero et al. 2012). A highly illustrative example of this is the complete rewrite which Russian school textbooks of Russian history underwent in the wake of the fall of the Soviet Union, giving new meaning to the phrase 'politically correct' curricular content (Zadja 2017: 22).

Case example 9.5:

The sounds of silence: American history textbook representations of non-violence and the Abolition Movement (Stoskopf and Bermudez 2017)

Context: This study joins together previous work done in the fields of history education and peace studies. Scholarship has shown the important role played by an extensive network of peaceful groups dedicated to the abolition of slavery by non-violent means.

Goal: To examine the portrayal of the tactics of the Abolition Movement in four popular American history textbooks.

Outcomes: The four textbooks present the Abolition Movement in varying degrees as being responsible for a climate of social violence which led to the American Civil War. The use of peaceful and non-violent means is silenced by the presentation of the narrative in the textbooks, and this obscures an important part of this period of history from the readers of the textbooks. The researchers argue that this skews not only student understanding of the Abolition Movement, but also of the role of non-violent protest more widely. They also argue that equipping students with the analytical tools to understand how ideological messages are conveyed through the construction of knowledge is an empowering act for them.

Methods: The researchers made a purposeful selection of a sample of textbooks based on information about textbook uptake, selected for some diversity of reading level and also based on their self-presentation. The analysis focused on the use of specific discursive practices to convey ideological messages to the reader, whether through implicit or explicit means. The researchers identify three particular devices to be the focus of their analysis: narrative framing, positioning and stance.

While analysis of written texts (see Chapter 10) can be particularly fruitful for considering the nature of knowledge and truth claims which are made, this is also an interesting topic for the analysis of spoken language in classroom discourse. Both how teachers construct narratives to teach specific knowledge content and the things that students will accept as knowledge are worthy of investigation. A combination of the two, to act on the suggestions of Stoskopf and Bermudez (2017), to explicitly teach students to analyse how knowledge is constructed in textbooks through discursive practices, and to explore how they understand the nature of the task, might be particularly interesting. This pedagogical approach is the one known as critical literacy, which has been critiqued as lacking in a knowledge base by those who are proponents of the cultural literacy movement.

A further critical view of knowledge is one that asserts the ways in which we think about and understand knowledge in education research have been dictated by a dominant (Western) philosophical tradition and that different cultures have different epistemologies and understandings of how knowledge is constructed. An example which has been widely debated is the concept of plagiarism and whether in some cultures the use of authorities and a tissue of intertextual quotation to build up an argument is simply the respectful and appropriate way to write, rather than an act of intellectual theft (Liu 2005). This is a highly contested and debated field, but may be of interest to those working in multicultural or multinational contexts; suggested further reading is given at the end of this chapter. The idea is perhaps more acceptable in education where we can see the influence that the differing intellectual traditions in different subject areas have had on how knowledge and knowing are conceptualized (e.g. Svendson and Svendson 2016).

Conclusion

In this chapter we have considered a variety of different ways that knowledge and knowing is conceptualized in education and in discourse research, which often vary between different subject areas, drawing on different traditions of epistemology. The approach taken by different researchers can depend on their subject origins as well as their methodological preferences, and we have given examples of a wide range of different possibilities.

We have also mentioned some critical approaches to the idea of knowledge in education. These align with wider societal concerns which are highly current as we write this, and which we suspect will continue to be so for some time: post-truth and fake news are two concepts which we have not mentioned but which are deeply relevant to the lives students will go on to after their classroom experience.

Knowledge is at the heart of the educational endeavour, but we hope that we have in this chapter demonstrated that it is not as simple as it might at first seem. How claims to knowledge are made and underwritten by teachers and students; what 'facts' are presented by textbooks or how new knowledge is assimilated into old are just a few of the ways in which you might choose to research knowledge in classroom discourse.

Further Reading

Mercer, N. (2002), 'Researching common knowledge: Studying the content and context of educational discourse', in G. Walford (ed.), *Doing educational research*, 53–70, Abingdon, OX: Routledge. This chapter is a provocation of a different sort about knowledge and research in classroom discourse: What are you actually trying to know and why does it matter?

Nichols, T. (2017), *The death of expertise: The campaign against established knowledge and why it matters*, New York: Oxford University Press. This is a book written for a popular audience on the role of knowledge within society today, and how we view it. It provides a wide-ranging look at the implications of some of the issues we have raised in this chapter.

Ruitenberg, C.W, and D.C. Phillips, eds (2011), *Education, culture and epistemological diversity: Mapping a disputed terrain* (Vol. 2), New York: Springer Science and Business Media. This book explores the question of how different cultures can have different epistemologies and understandings of how and what knowledge is, and the debates around this question.

CHAPTER TEN

Written Texts

Introduction

While most researchers of classroom discourse are interested in spoken language, there are also rich areas of research in written texts, which can draw on several of the approaches covered in Part One. This chapter considers the different sources of written data, and some of the research which has been done using them. In research methods literature the analysis of written documents is often called 'documentary analysis'. Written texts can be naturally occurring or they can be the result of deliberate tasks given to generate data on a particular topic. The world of education is awash in written texts; no classroom is without them, whether they are in the form of textbooks and children's work, or the curriculum documents which guide what take place within that classroom. Schools are constantly generating more written documents on policies, or to comply with external demands, or to communicate within their staff. This vast range means that written texts can provide a wealth of data for the educational researcher.

Constructed texts

One of the key things to remember with written data is that it can be more crafted than spoken discourse. 'Documents are not neutral, transparent reflections of organisational or occupational life' (Atkinson and Coffey 2010: 77). They have usually been written with a specific purpose and audience in mind, which means that they have been constructed in a particular way. Take, for example, a school assessment and feedback policy, which might have a principal audience of the staff in the school, and a purpose of getting them to act in a particular way. But it might also have a principal audience of parents and school inspectors – with a purpose of demonstrating compliance or good practice. It might also have an audience of parents and children with a purpose of allowing staff to defend themselves from accusations that they are not marking work frequently enough – because they are acting in accordance with the policy. In each case the construction of the written document would be subtly different. It is rare for spoken discourse to be this considered, although it sometimes is.

When working with written discourse it is important to remember it is constructed; case example 10.2 talks about the problem of using children's essays as evidence of 'truth' about a historical period, but they can still provide interesting data for analysis. In that particular case the analysis considers the ways that the children draw on dominant discourses from the time, including popular songs, to present themselves in a particular way. In that case the audience was not just the schoolteacher but the government, who set the essay question as part of a survey of public morale, so the children were writing with a sense of a higher authority – just as students do now when they are writing in an examination. Scott (1990) suggests there are four things that we need to think about when dealing with documentary sources for social science research: *authenticity* (is it real? Has it been altered?), *credibility* (is it accurate? Does it tell the truth?), *representativeness* (why has this document survived? Is there a bias in the type of document which has not survived?) and *meaning* (the interpretation of the content). These apply to a greater or lesser extent depending on the source of the text you are working with.

What data?

'Classroom discourse' as written data can come in many forms. Textbooks, school schemes of work, government policies, examination specifications, examination papers, course handbooks, online resources, children's written work in exercise books or in examination conditions, and any other number of other artefacts come under this heading. Interesting studies can be done on many of these written texts. The case examples in this chapter are of studies involving a study edition of a favourite school novel (*Of Mice and Men*); classroom exercises generated for the purpose by history teachers looking at the effect of genre in history tasks; examination specifications from across the UK and some essays written in 1942 by schoolgirls during the Blitz, which have recently been analysed. They could just as easily have been of government policy documents, speeches given by Betsy DeVos or Michael Gove (which are treated as written text because they are usually issued as official documents), or studies of representation of race and gender in the examples in mathematics textbooks.

In general there are two types of written texts that can be considered 'classroom discourse'; those produced by students (and teachers) within the classroom (or as homework), and the rest, which are typically published or more or less publicly available (but include things like schemes of work which are internal to the school). These are all 'classroom discourse' because they all contribute to the *discourses* which meet in the classroom space: they guide the emphasis that is placed on assessment, for example, or define what subject content is used, or who is represented within the curriculum. Case example 10.1 shows how this works. Mason and Giovanelli (2017) analysed a popular educational edition of *Of Mice and Men*; the notes and guiding questions in the book contribute or even dictate what lines of enquiry and discussion take place in the classroom in relation to the text. The content of the edition outside of the novel text itself all enter into the interaction between text, child and teacher, and thus form an important part of classroom discourse.

Case example 10.1:

What do you think? Let me tell you: Discourse about texts and the literature classroom (Mason and Giovanelli 2017)

Context: A critical stylistic analysis of a popular edition of John Steinbeck's *Of Mice and Men*.

Goal: To examine how reading a text in a literature classroom is framed by the use of educational editions, and how this might affect students' experience and understanding of studying fiction.

Outcomes: The article uses detailed stylistic analysis of the first and last between-chapter study guides from a specific edition to explore how students' attention and potentially therefore their understanding is directed towards specific information and interpretation. The notes sections, the authors point out, are placed before rather than after chapters; they comprise a summary of what is about to happen, and some pointers to guide reading in the next chapter. Readers therefore encounter the text *after* they have been exposed to discourse about it, and they will also be asked questions which they cannot answer at the moment at which they are asked. These questions, the authors show, are framed so as to direct the reader to particular answers. The authors argue that their analysis suggests an emphasis on the 'learning *content*' rather than the 'responding *to texts*' approach to the study of English literature.

Methods: The study used a close stylistic analysis of the contents of the first and last notes sections in a popular educational edition of *Of Mice and Men*. These sections were chosen to be representative of the edition as a whole, but also to provide a way to examine how student responses were framed at the supposed beginning and end of reading. They use a linguistic and interpretative qualitative analysis, looking at what ideologies might be embedded in the text, and what that suggests about the approach to reading literary texts in the classroom. Because the stylistic analysis looks to examine ideologies, it is a critical stylistic approach (Jeffries 2008). The article draws on schema theory to discuss the ways in which knowledge is organized as we acquire it.

Why use written texts as data?

Written data is significantly easier to obtain and process for analysis than spoken data particularly if it is in printed form; it can also be significantly cheaper when considering the costs of data collection and transcription. It is also useful in that the data is readily inspected by others who want to confirm your findings. However, the most important thing to consider is what question you want to answer with your research when choosing written or spoken data – or both.

Written data can be very helpful for scene setting for an investigation which goes on to record classroom discussion. You might conduct a content analysis of an examination specification (like that in case example 10.3) as a starting point in exploring the role of certain materials in the curriculum – in the case example, books by women. We concur with Prior (2013) that written texts are not peripheral but are valuable and relevant data sources in their own right.

Your study might also require the contextualization of written documents; an analysis of a textbook in RE, for example, might provide the necessary context for analysing student attitudes towards atheism in a classroom discussion. Without the right context a researcher could mistake the source of a student's view which might alter their conclusions.

Written and spoken data together can also help with 'triangulation' – finding different ways of providing answers to the same question, which can help to confirm, complement or complicate them. Sundaram and Sauntson (2016), for example, looked at 'discursive silences' around the idea of pleasure in sex and relationships education in England. They did so by combining CDA of government guidance around sex and relationships education with analysis of focus group discussions with young women. The two together helped to triangulate the way that sex is constructed by and for teenage girls as 'risky' and specifically with gendered expectations around pleasure. One or the other data source would have produced an incomplete picture; by bringing the two together they were able to show both the understandings of the teens and how those were partially created by sex and relationships education policy. While we have covered mainly qualitative approaches in this book (with the notable exception of corpus linguistics in Chapter 6) written texts might also feature as a preliminary stage in a 'mixed methods' study where a quantitative phase followed.

Defining your corpus

Before starting to analyse texts, it is necessary to define exactly what your data set is. A class set of essays on civic values? Or all their essays from the term's study of citizenship? If you are looking at government policy on a certain topic, will you look at policy statements made by the political party while they were campaigning for election, or only once elected? How many years' worth will you look at? What counts as a 'government' document? When Victoria, with another researcher, was researching the way food and young people were constructed in government documents, they included, as well as speeches and government statements, both newspaper articles written by government ministers in their capacity as ministers and also a report which was written by people who were actually restaurant owners, but which had been sponsored and directed by government policy (Elliott and Hore 2016). This was a deliberate choice to provide a wider and more interesting data set, but the decision was justified with reference to the ultimate source of the document.

Decisions about which documents to use are made with reference to the research questions that need to be answered. Alternatively, a particular document, such as textbook, might prompt a research question; seeing a stereotypical French man on a bicycle with a garland of onions and a stripy jumper might suggest a research question around the presentation of French people in that textbook more generally.

If you are conducting an analysis of students' work, it is useful to think about what is best for your purposes. Are naturally occurring data such as classwork or course essays likely to have enough of whatever it is you are looking for? Or are they better because they are natural, and not steered in a particular direction by having been created for a special purpose? On the other hand, if you are investigating their understanding of a particular concept, you may need a specific stimulus to make sure that there is enough data for you to work from, without having to analyse a whole term's worth of classwork.

Case example 10.2:

'Till we hear the last all clear': Gender and the presentation of self in young girls' writing about the bombing of Hull during the Second World War (Greenhalgh 2014)

Context: A study of essays written by Hull schoolgirls about their experiences of air raids in 1942.

Goal: To examine the ways in which gender and presentation of self become evident in twenty-nine essays written by ten- to twelve-year-old girls in response to the question 'What happened to me and what I did in the air raids'.

Outcomes: The essays suggest attempts by the writers to present themselves as composed and maintaining morale, which the author suggests may be linked to the essay stimulus coming from a central government survey. Despite articulations of fear, the essays are determinedly cheerful. There are high levels of first person plural pronouns, suggesting a communal view. The author also highlights the use of phrases and titles from popular songs as tools to express stoicism. The schoolgirls position their roles strongly in line with those of their mothers, as apprentices to their domestic and civilian responsibilities. The discourses in the essays suggest a heavy emphasis on good morale as a civilian virtue, and also their adherence to stratified notions of gender roles.

Methods: This is a historical discourse analysis, which understands the narratives of the girls as utilizing a number of constructs 'selected from the dominant discourses available to them' (Greenhalgh 2014: 169). It is a qualitative analysis, which looks closely at the narratives in the essays and uses them to reconstruct general discourses, and to connect with popular cultural references, such as wartime songs, with a particular focus on gender distinctions in the ways the girls present themselves and others in their essays.

When defining your corpus it is thus important to consider the focus of your research, the available quantity of data as well as the relevance and authenticity of the source.

Content analysis

Content analysis is a primarily quantitative methodology which is often used with written texts. Case example 10.3 is an example of a content analysis which Victoria did, albeit a very simple one. The simplicity in this case highlighted a striking imbalance in the texts set in the curriculum in the UK, more than a more complex analysis might have done.

Case example 10.3:

Gender and the contemporary educational canon in the UK (Elliott 2017)

Context: A study of the gender balance in English Literature set texts for sixteen-year-olds in the UK.

Goal: To examine the representation of female authors and characters within the educational canon of the UK.

Outcomes: There is a very heavy imbalance in favour of male authors and characters in the set texts for examination in the UK; with two-thirds of text options being by male authors. Heritage texts are more likely to have a higher representation of female authors; modern drama texts which are set are least likely to be by women. The situation is particularly bad in Northern Ireland where there was just one novel by a woman on the syllabus. The article argues that despite an opportunity for change given by a reform of examination specifications in some of the countries of the UK, a sense of inertia is created by the desire for texts which already have a large amount of resources available to support their teaching.

Methods: The study was a content analysis of examination specifications from the exam boards in the UK. Excluding Shakespeare and poetry, the analysis involved a count of all the male and female authored texts, and an identification of the sex of the main character of each text. Different sorts of texts (pre-1900, drama, modern texts) were analysed separately. This was a simple count analysis which was used to investigate the content of the 'hidden curriculum' (Deem 1978: 46). It was motivated from a feminist critical point of view, which informed the framing and interpretation of results.

Other content analyses might include counting the number of times a particular term (or set of terms) comes up, or the number of categories of adjectives used to describe certain people or objects. Once a simple content analysis has been done, the quantitative data produced can be used for more complicated statistical analyses. It can be useful for examining trends over time. Bebell and Stemler (2004), for example, looked at the mission statements of a random set of schools in Massachusetts before and five years after the implementation of high-stakes state assessments. They found that schools that had changed their mission statements in that time had increased references to the cognitive purposes of schooling, while references to physical education, citizenship or socio-emotional development had diminished.

Content analysis can be done on a large scale, as with corpus linguistics. Automated or computer-driven content analysis has increased in popularity in recent years. Among other less glamorous applications, it is content analysis that demonstrated J. K. Rowling to be the author of the Robert Galbraith crime novel *Cuckoo Calling*; according to an article in *Smithsonian* magazine it took Patrick Juola, a Computer Science professor at Duquesne University, just 30 minutes to conclude that Rowling was Galbraith, using a computer-driven content analysis (Zax 2014). If this is an area that interests you, suggested further reading is given at the end of the chapter.

Scoring written data – rubrics and reliability

We discussed thematic and discourse analysis in Chapter 4, and these methods are often used with written texts. However, classroom research with children's work often uses methods of assessment which are familiar to teachers all over the world, and makes a judgement based on written work. This is particularly so when the written work is being used as a test of the effectiveness of a particular change, or as evidence of particular learning, practices or views on the part of students.

This section deals with the question of generating 'rubrics' – the instructions for how to make a judgement – and the question of ensuring reliability of scoring. Case example 10.4 demonstrates the use of a rubric produced for a research project, as the researchers were interested in the ways in which students transformed the information from historical sources in their own writing, and so they needed a specific form of analysis to provide a 'score', which they then used for a statistical analysis. In this case they defined four types of statement that represented transformations from the source material. Each of these was defined by the researchers so that they had a clear idea what each term meant and if they were scoring the essays in the study correctly – essential for a study which was using experimental methods and a statistical analysis of the scores.

Case example 10.4:

Effects of genre and content knowledge on historical thinking with academically diverse high school Students (De La Paz and Wissinger 2015)

Context: A study of the genres of writing high school students are asked to do in history.

Goal: To examine whether being asked to write argument or summary influences students' understanding of sources, and how their prior content knowledge affects this understanding and writing.

Outcomes: The study suggests that the genre of writing (summary vs. argument) has a very limited effect on student's ability to read and write from primary sources. Prior content knowledge had the greatest effect. The authors suggest that their results show it is more important to the development of historical thinking to ask students to consider both sides when studying a contentious event, and to provide evidence from source material, than to pick either argument or summary writing. Students with special educational needs showed an equal ability to think historically when provided with appropriate accommodations such as support in reading source material.

Methods: The study involved 101 eleventh-grade students in US history courses in Pennsylvania, of whom 10 per cent had special educational needs. The authors used an experimental design where students were randomly assigned to take part in either an argument or a summary task in a topic on the Gulf of Tonkin using primary sources. Students' content knowledge was measured on a multiple choice test, and they completed a reading comprehension test as well as the writing task and a psychometric test of writing ability. Essays were coded using procedures from Wiley and Voss (1999), which required students' writing to be segmented into 'idea units'. These idea units were divided into four categories: paraphrases, elaborations, additions, or misconceptions and points awarded accordingly (elaborations scored 2 as being the most transformed use of source material; misconceptions were scored negatively). A number of other 'rubrics' or scoring guides were also used. A subset of essays were scored by someone who did not know which groups the students were in, with a high level of agreement.

One reason why it is important to have a rubric is the need to ensure terms and definitions are pinned down. See O'Hallaron and Schleppegrell (2016) for an example of the difficulty of the term 'voice' in assessing students' writing in science lessons. The authors also highlight the fact that some words mean different things in different subjects so if you are conducting a collaborative research project with more than one subject represented it becomes doubly important to make sure your definitions are clear. 'Evaluate', for example, means something very different in mathematics than it does in history.

It is important to consider what you are interested in finding out when considering ways in which to write instructions for scoring written work (something which we might refer to as content validity – are you really measuring what you want to measure?). Take the example of the use of terminology in geography students' essays. One approach would simply be to count the number of technical terms students included in their essays. But you might also want to differentiate between correct and appropriate use or incorrect use. You might also want to think about the density of terms – that is, the number of terms used per hundred words (for example) which would require you to count the number of words altogether. You might also decide that some terms were more advanced than others, so value them more highly. It is important to think carefully about the different possibilities in even quite a simple piece of analysis, and to consider exactly what it is you want to measure. Spelling is another challenging feature to score. In England the National Curriculum Tests, which ended in 2008, had four points allocated for spelling. Rather than simply having a count of the number of spelling errors, the assessment rubric asked markers to consider what level of vocabulary was being used – for example, simple, complex regular or complex irregular, and then think about whether the vocabulary was spelled right, in which case reduce the score given by one mark from the level of the vocabulary. This prevented unambitious writers getting better marks for spelling than those who tried for difficult words but did not manage them. These are just examples, but they demonstrate the need to think carefully about the way that textual analysis can support your research question and ultimately your claims.

One popular form of textual analysis is error analysis, particularly in L2 or EFL teaching. It often takes a similar approach to case example 10.4, in that errors are categorized in different forms. If this is a form of research that interests you, then see Jobeen et al. (2015) for an example of this kind of analysis of written data. It can be a particularly useful tool for teaching in that it has a strong element of formative assessment about it.

You might also decide simply to use a ready-made scoring system; perhaps using a mark scheme provided by an examination board, or agreed grading criteria in your school, will provide you with the right kind of judgement for the research question in which you are interested. Even in these cases, and in all cases where you have generated a rubric yourself, you should consider the question of reliability. All teachers are aware of the potential mismatch between different grades applying putatively the same mark scheme to the same material!

Reliability in the context of research means two things: it means if two people analysed the same piece of data independently would they do the same thing with it; and if the same person analysed the same piece of data twice with a gap of time in between would they do the same thing with it both times? Having sufficiently clear instructions about how to make judgements of students' work is essential for producing reliability in this kind of textual research. To check your own consistency over time is relatively easy: simply choose a small portion of your sample and apply your rubric to a clean copy. Inter-rater reliability matters most if there is more than one person working on the data analysis. Sometimes researchers who are working alone will ask a colleague to apply the rubric to a small sample of written work to ensure that the way they are interpreting it makes sense. If more than one researcher is rating work according to a rubric then it is possible to do a statistical analysis of agreement (such as Cohen's Kappa [see Wood 2007]); you might find it more useful to discuss where disagreements have formed and work out why they have. If you are using normal mark schemes or grading criteria it is a sensible idea to have everything graded by two different people and to use the average.

Multimodal texts

Multimodal research considers the things that go along with language – written or spoken – as essential components of the way that meaning is made. Kress defines mode as 'a socially shaped and culturally given resource for meaning making' (2009: 54). This could be music, a gesture, an image, a gif, an emoticon, the layout of a text; or even, the words on the page! One way in which many cultures and sources use multimodal approaches is through the symbolism of colour; the association of green with Islam, the colour black with death or the use of the rainbow in relation to LGBTQ+, for example.

A school textbook is almost certainly a multimodal text: it is likely to have pictures or highlighted text, diagrams, etc. Multimodal analysis considers the ways in which meaning is made by those elements as well as by the words that are written on the page. **Consider** this sentence. Is the meaning different because of the emboldened word? We would argue it is. Thinking about that difference in meaning is multimodal analysis. In a multimodal text all of the 'modes' – the elements of the text – combine to create the meaning of the text, that is, what is communicated by it (Kress et al. 2001). The way the meanings of the different elements relate and combine is called 'intersemiotic relations'. (See Jewitt 2009 for a detailed set of theoretical concepts that are used in multimodal research.)

Although some multimodal analysis is highly technical, it is possible to do it without getting mired in the field of semiotics. You might ask, for example, why a text has been put in Comic Sans, or what the apparent target age of the illustrations in a text book is and how that ties in with the text. To give an example of how you might think about multimodal texts, picture 10.1 is an image of half a page from an article which we wrote on wait time in the classroom (Ingram and Elliott 2016).

The figure presents the same information as in the written text, in a visual way. However, the shape of the figure also resembles the symbol of the smiley face. This, analysis might suggest, evokes a friendly tone; perhaps it is intended to make the ideas within the text seem easier to process. Or perhaps you might view the use of the symbol as patronising, given that the article in question is intended to be a practice based one, with applications for teachers in the classroom. You might also, if you have the right level of cynicism, correctly interpret the use of this figure as an attempt to be a memorable journal article, that people might refer to as the 'smiley face paper', and thus a more widely known paper. To our regret, no one has yet referred to it as that except us!

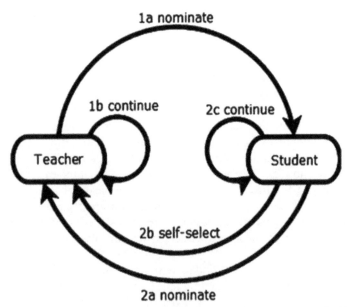

FIGURE 10.1 *An exemplar of a multimodal text from Ingram and Elliott (2016: 41).*

These different possibilities illustrate one of the difficulties of multimodal analysis, namely that meaning is even more open to interpretation in non-written communication, and even more dependent on the particular understandings of the reader.

You will want to consider the multimodal elements of texts where the meaning of the modes other than language makes a significant difference to the meaning of the text. If you are conducting any research which includes both spoken language and another source of information, such as pupils' books or the diagrams on the whiteboard, then you are drawing on multimodal source material. The most common source of multimodal material in society today, however, is the internet, where text, emoticons, pictures, gifs, videos, audio, animations and many more can be combined in the production of a single page of 'text'.

Conclusion

Written texts are easy to acquire, although researchers have to make decisions about the limits of the data set. They can form useful background or contextual data to a study of spoken language, or help researchers to triangulate their findings for a more accurate picture. They can also provide valuable research insights on their own, and many researchers only work with written texts. Critical approaches as discussed in Chapter 4 can be applied to written texts, but they can also be analysed in more straightforward ways. We have introduced content analysis here, and also suggested the idea of thematic analysis which we have not covered in this book.

It is worth considering the range of written texts which might be relevant to your research topic even if you think your primary data will be spoken. We have mentioned triangulation and contextualization but the prime reason for thinking about the written texts that relate to your topic is the potential to strengthen the claims that you are able to make from your research. Only CA of the theoretical and methodological approaches we mentioned in Part One would reject written texts. There are some ethical considerations to think about in relation to written data, if you are asking students to produce them especially for your study, but pupils' written work can be one of the most valuable sources of information if you are interested in the ways in learning is happening or being shown.

Further reading

Fitzgerald, T. (2012), 'Documents and documentary analysis', in A. R. Briggs, M. Morrison and M. Coleman (eds), *Research methods in educational leadership and management*, 296–308, London: SAGE. A further introduction to the methods of documentary analysis and the ways of managing documents as data.

Neuendorf, K. A. (2016). *The content analysis guidebook*, Thousand Oaks, CA: SAGE. A full methodology for conducting content analysis.

Scott, J. (1990) *A matter of record: Documentary sources in social research*, Cambridge: Polity Press. A broad-ranging and useful, if old, book on the use of documents in social science.

Practical Considerations

Introduction to Part Three

Part Three's chapters offer three different areas of practical concern to researchers of classroom discourse: ethics, data collection and transcription decisions. Although the details of each of these areas will vary according to the particular theoretical approach that you have chosen for your research, issues specific to the theoretical approaches we cover have been included in each of those earlier chapters. Here we cover more general issues which have relevance for researchers using a variety of methods; these have implications for the decisions that you will need to make early in the research process.

Chapter 11 delves further into the complexities of ethical decisions as they relate to research in classroom discourse. We discuss problems rather than procedures, and raise a number of questions which you may need to think about when planning research in educational contexts, whether or not you are affiliated to a university with institutional ethics protocols such as an IRB in the United States or ethics committees in the UK. There will be considerable differences in the decisions that need to be made by different researchers, given that many issues are unique to the context in which you are researching.

Chapter 12 considers the practicalities of collecting data for classroom discourse research, including decisions around the use of audio and video equipment. We discuss questions of sampling to select participants, the quality and nature of data that you need to collect, and how this is always related back to the focus of your research questions. We also urge you to consider how much data you want or need to generate: too much data provides just as many challenges as too little. Technically, what is commonly called data collection is actually 'data generation' in that by making the recording you are creating the data. When you engage with this chapter you will need to think about your specific context and how your participants will respond to different approaches to data collection and generation.

Chapter 13 concludes this section by considering the different ways in which spoken data can be transcribed. We treat transcription as part of the analytic, decision-making process and offer a range of options and issues for you to consider. While some theoretical approaches dictate certain methods of transcription, in other cases the detail that is required is related to your research design and once again the question of how much data you can actually analyse. This chapter also addresses the differences between transcribing for the purpose of analysis and transcribing for the purpose of dissemination.

CHAPTER ELEVEN

Ethics

Introduction

Researching in schools carries particular ethical implications and responsibilities; this chapter explores some of the issues which researchers need to consider when designing their studies of classroom discourse. This includes the storage and publication of data, as well as their initial collection. If you are conducting research as part of a university then you will have strict ethical guidelines and procedures to follow from that university, which will differ according to your national context and institution. If you are conducting research purely in the context of your role as a teacher, then you have the responsibility to act ethically. This chapter raises some of the practical and ethical considerations you face as a researcher of classroom discourse or as a teacher/researcher. The further reading at the end of this chapter suggests the ethical codes from both the British and the American Educational Research Associations, which can help you consider all the different issues and act as a responsible ethical researcher.

Acting ethically versus ethical procedures

Most schools will have their own procedures in relation to the ethics and permission for carrying out research on site; all universities will also have ethical procedures which you are required to follow if you are associated with them. Ethical research is not merely a matter of procedures, however. Ethics is an ongoing process that asks you to think about participants and to act in an ethically appropriate fashion at each stage of the research process. This chapter raises some of the procedural issues but also some of the more important ethical dilemmas and issues for researchers working in schools, particularly if they themselves are teachers. It is important to remember that 'ethics is not something to be forgotten once "ethics approval" has been gained but, instead, needs to inform all of our actions as education researchers' (Brooks et al. 2014: 3). Even more so if you are working in a context where you do not need to gain 'ethics approval'.

One of the key ethical questions to ask yourself is what the effect of taking part in your research will be for the students or teachers who are your participants. In relation to research where teachers are changing something in their practice in particular, to be ethical means to be confident that the change will at least be no worse than the status quo. Some researchers have argued that the social value of research is a key indicator of quality: research needs to do some 'good' in the world (e.g. Oancea and Furlong 2005; Ortega 2005). For most educators, this is not a problematic hurdle to clear; most people looking to do research in classroom discourse are interested to know what is happening for the purpose of improving teaching and learning in their classrooms and more widely.

Getting permission

All research involving human subjects works on the principle of 'informed consent' – that is, that in order to give permission to a researcher to use their data, a participant must have a good understanding of what the study involves. The age at which students are considered able to give informed consent varies between countries. Most students will be too young to give consent on their own, and will need parental consent for involvement in research, where the activities they will be taking part in are outside normal practice for the school. Nevertheless most researchers would consider it unethical to only gain parental consent and to (for example) record a child's participation where that child was not happy to take part. Researchers often refer to 'assent' rather than 'consent' in relation to children. Some schools will have systems in place that allow for 'opt out' consent rather than 'opt in'. For 'opt out' consent parents are sent information about the study and what it will involve for their child and are asked to get in touch with the teacher if they do not want their child to take part. This kind of consent is usually far easier for whole-class studies, as with 'opt in' it can be hard to get a permission slip back from every parent.

Some schools will have policies in place which parents sign up to at the time of admission which allow for the filming or audio recording of students as part of teachers' professional development activities. If your school has this policy, then it is important to check that it will enable you to do everything you want with the data, such as using extracts in school to work with other teachers, using extracts and conclusions out of school to present your findings, publishing your findings including extracts of data, and keeping and storing the data. If not, you will need to gain extra permission. In terms of what you are recording, if what you are asking students to do is within the realm of what you might do anyway as a classroom teacher, such as setting up a whole-class debate, or getting them to work in groups to solve a particular problem, then you do not need explicit permission to do this, only to record the event, or get them to fill in contextual information questionnaires (for example). If you are planning on analysing students' written work, if it is something they would have been producing anyway, that is within normal teaching practice. If you plan to use extracts from their work in public, however, good practice is to get consent.

Flewitt (case example 11.1) points out the problems of 'informed consent' in the context of exploratory research which does not have a fixed path to follow (2006). This is often the case in studies of classroom discourse which might be designed to follow the most interesting issue that arises in the course of data collection. She suggests thinking of consent as 'provisional' and ongoing, so that you should continually consider how you are affecting your participants through your research and consider ethical issues as they arise.

Case example 11.1

Using video to investigate preschool classroom interaction: Education research assumptions and methodological practices (Flewitt 2006)

Context: This draws on an ethnographic video case study of three-year-olds communicating at home and in a preschool playgroup.

Goal: To use multimodal data (i.e. not just spoken language) to understand the long-standing phenomenon of different perceptions of the same child in different social settings (and the fact that they talk far less at preschool than at home).

Outcomes: The article demonstrates the need for the inclusion of non-verbal communication in studies of preschool children and also presents some resulting methodological and ethical issues. Using video data is particularly problematic for anonymity, which it is important to retain for small children. Flewitt suggests pixellation or outline drawings as a way to use data publically. The study demonstrated that by including transcription, or 'representation' (p. 36) of the non-verbal body movement and gaze data gathered on film, a much more accurate picture of the communicative abilities of a child even when they make no verbal utterances can be created. There are, however, difficulties of representing all the complexity of multimodal, dynamic data within a complete and systematized scheme of transcription, because of the sheer volume.

Methods: This was a longitudinal study of three-year-olds at home and preschool using video, audio and written methods of data collection, in order to allow triangulation of evidence, but also to explore the range of communicative resources which young children can use in addition to spoken language, including noises, gaze, facial expressions and movement.

The principle of informed consent also applies to your colleagues if you are going to record their classrooms as well as your own. Consent can always be withdrawn so if someone agrees that you can record their lesson then decides at the last minute – or after – that they would rather not have their lesson included in your research then you must respect that decision however frustrating it is. You will need to consider in this situation what data can or cannot be used. In general all data collected from the withdrawn participant is deleted, but what will you do if it is already published or it has already been part of the analysis?

Unequal power relations

One of the critical issues for the teacher-researcher is the unequal power relations between a researcher and her participants, which is reinforced by the unequal power of a teacher and her students. This power differential has practical implications in that it can affect the data. For example, students can feel the need to please the teacher by altering their responses or behaviour to reflect what they think the teacher would like. It also has ethical implications as students can feel unable to refuse their participation in data collection. Case example 11.2 uses discourse data to illustrate a question of teacher authority.

Case example 11.2:

Authority, power and morality in classroom discourse (Buzzelli and Johnston 2001)

Context: This paper uses an extract of classroom data to explore Bernstein's concept of pedagogic discourse (1996) within a third-grade writing classroom in the United States.

Goal: To explore interrelated questions of morality, authority and power in classroom discourse, given that teacher authority is always present.

Outcomes: The teacher and the children discuss the use of the word 'beer' in one of the children's stories, and the appropriateness of that. The authors use this discussion to highlight the double nature of pedagogic discourse: there is the 'instructional discourse' which has a 'function of developing competencies' and the 'regulative discourse' with a function 'to maintain social order, manner and conduct' (2001: 882), and the teacher has to balance each of them. Although this teacher leads the children to discuss and reject the use of 'beer' as socially inappropriate themselves, the authors suggest there are no right or wrong ways to handle this kind of dilemma. They highlight the fact that classroom discourse is always in the context of power and moral constraints.

Methods: This is a largely theoretical article which uses an extract of a lesson on writing with third graders to give a practical example of the concepts it has raised. The transcription is focused on content and features the teacher and seven students.

Teachers have authority in classroom discourse whether they choose to enforce it or not; a correlated point is that power relations in the classroom are always unequal (Buzzelli and Johnston 2001). Think about ways in which you can mitigate the power difference – you might want to interview children in pairs or small groups, for example, or you may need to find a form of words that emphasizes you are interested in their opinions and views and will not take anything they say personally. Would it be better to have someone else interview your students?

When conducting research using classroom discourse data the unequal power relations are one of the points of interest, and something which explains how conversation in the classroom works. This is sometimes represented by researchers in the Conversation Analytic tradition by giving teachers male names and pupils female names in transcripts, unless gender is otherwise made relevant. The famous IRE sequence depends on the authority of the teacher for its framing. Our own research has explored the ways in which the teacher always holds the power of nomination of a speaker in a traditional classroom environment (Ingram and Elliott 2014). So the unequal power relations between teachers and students are a fact of life, not a critique of classroom research. It is important to mitigate them when gaining informed consent, and to reassure students there are no 'right' or 'wrong' answers or behaviours when you are involving them in research, but in terms of data analysis we have to acknowledge the power imbalance and consider its effect on the data.

You should also be aware of unequal power relations as they apply to your colleagues. If you are a head of department wanting to record your department members' lessons, for example, or a member of the school's senior leadership or management team, that has ethical implications both in terms of the teachers' ability to refuse you and also the possibility that they will feel vulnerable at your watching their lesson or criticizing their practice. The opposite may also be true – would a senior leader feel happy at being observed/recorded by a recently qualified teacher looking at questioning strategies? They might not! Again you may need to think of ways to mitigate this imbalance in power depending on your role. Similarly if you ask for volunteers for research via a headteacher (whether in your own school or not) you are setting up particular power differentials and challenges for recruitment. You may also have to offer assurances about being able to keep participants' identities confidential and separate from any findings you are going to report back.

Awareness of critical issues – the silencing of groups

Some researchers argue that we have a duty to do 'emancipatory' educational research; that is, that we should be using our power as teachers and researcher to give a voice to those who might usually be silenced by school and societal structures (Cameron et al. 2018). This might include, for example, students who experience difficulties, in the UK categorized as those with Special Educational Needs. Often researchers do not include these students in studies because of the risk of harm (or because of the difficulty of gaining access through gatekeepers) so they are less likely to have their views represented. Ethical research in relation to these groups might include making sure that they are represented in your participants even if they are not your specific research focus.

However, classroom discourse research can also be used to explore norms that operate in schools to silence certain groups. Case example 11.3 shows an example of a particular critical issue in the classroom: that of race. It reflects the use of close examination of classroom talk to consider the difficulties surrounding talking about race in the classroom, even when the object of study is a novel with foregrounded racial issues. This was a study with a particular ethical drive: to examine closely issues of why it is difficult to talk about race, and what implications this may have for staff and students.

Case study 11.3

'We Always Talk about Race': Navigating race talk dilemmas in the teaching of literature (Thomas 2015)

Context: This study explores the difficulty of talking about race in a racially diverse classroom when the teaching of literature promotes a discussion of race in the text that mirrors or challenges contemporary race relations. It uses data from a larger discourse analysis study in which seven teachers recorded one class for an entire semester.

Goal: To look closely at the classroom talk of two veteran English teachers – an African American man and a white woman – in a racially diverse high school in the United States, showing how the teachers employ different strategies to navigate similarly difficult conversations, using an interactional ethnographic approach.

Outcomes: Both teachers were teaching novels with foregrounded racial issues, but dealt with these slightly differently interactionally. One placed boundaries around the use of a particular racial slur, while the other dealt directly with issues around the choice of racially focused literature. Silence and evasion still characterized conversations around the point of particularly fraught racial tensions, however. Both teachers and students can sometimes 'sidestep' race because it is so high in the potential for conflict. The authors point out that this reflects the complexity and tensions surrounding racial identity and history in the United States.

Methods: The interactional ethnographic approach is used to investigate race talk dilemmas which Thomas defines as 'moments in conversations about race that have the potential for conflict' (p. 155). The researcher had been a teacher at the school – a large Midwestern city comprehensive in the United States – and had returned to work as a researcher with the seven teachers in the larger study, teaching them how to use discourse analysis of their own classroom data. The study used a directed content analysis of videos that exemplified the dilemmas highlighted by the teacher; this sub-study used interactional ethnographic analysis of two lessons taught by different teachers who were each teaching a class of fifteen- and sixteen-year-olds. In addition to the two-hour-long lessons this study drew on study group interactions of the teachers and interviews with them. The transcripts were analysed specifically for a focus on the language of evaluation and judgement about how people did or ought to feel.

Critical research like that described in case example 11.3 seeks to make visible implicit power imbalances between groups of different races, genders or classes. It might be of particular interest to explore these issues where certain groups are under-attaining, for example. Movements to 'decolonize the curriculum' such as 'Why is my curriculum white?' and 'Rhodes must fall' in the United States and the United Kingdom also raise interesting possibilities to do with the material taught in school and university classrooms and its implications for those whose families were directly affected by the empire and colonization. Research driven by ethical considerations in this case might look like case example 11.3 but it might also be of the discourse generated by teaching that included acknowledgement of the ongoing repercussions of slavery today, for example.

The vulnerable participant

While undertaking critical research that might highlight injustices to participants that they were unaware of has the potential to harm as well as empower them, there are other groups who are vulnerable by virtue of the very characteristic that makes you want to research them. These may be the same as silenced groups – for example, children in care or children with a parent in prison – or it may be that the topic of your research is a sensitive one. Case example 11.4 illustrates one such sensitive topic, that of death.

Case study 11.4:

Dealing with the concepts of 'grief' and 'grieving' in the classroom: Children's perceptions, emotions and behaviour (Stylianou and Zembylas 2018)

Context: An action research study of an intervention to provide space for discussing death and dying in a class of ten- and eleven–year-old children in Cyprus.

Goal: To show how the students perceived death and dying and to explore the impact that the intervention had on their emotions and behaviour.

Outcomes: The students were able to define the term 'grief' after the intervention and used vocabulary that suggested a broad understanding of the term and the role of conflicting emotions about loss. Post interviews suggested that students were more able to articulate their own experiences of loss and had a richer vocabulary to do so. The intervention also offered children an opportunity to discuss death and grief independently with parents and with friends. The authors argue the intervention allowed the children to demystify the concepts of grief and grieving and that it was a pedagogically appropriate time and place to explore these concepts with students.

Methods: The action research intervention was a seven-phase programme of learning about death, grief and grieving, where each phase was one lesson of eighty minutes duration, with an additional eighty-minute lesson given to the phase of considering how grief was expressed by different people. The project took place over two cycles of action research (Kemmis and McTaggart 2005). The intervention was conducted with twenty students in an urban public primary school, where the main researcher was the classroom teacher. Informed consent was sought and gained from the parents of all of the children and sixteen of the children agreed to participate in pre and post interviews. No direct questions about experiences of grief were asked during these interviews although some children volunteered personal experiences. These interviews were analysed alongside notes taken relating to children's behaviour and body language during the interventions and children's written notes and drawings from the lessons throughout the intervention. Coding of all data was carried out deductively (from categories derived from the theoretical framework) and inductively (arising from the data). The article reports three main categories derived from this coding process: children's understandings of grief and grieving, their behaviour during the intervention programme and the ways in which their interpersonal behaviour changed during discussions of grief and grieving.

The ethical dilemmas that the authors of case example 11.4 highlight are to do with the pedagogical problems of teaching about grief and grieving in a context where the students may have different cultural and religious beliefs about them, where it is not known whether any of them have personal experience of death among close family members, or indeed where the teacher does not have enough technical knowledge to answer questions that may arise. However, were the study a slightly different one, to examine the construction of grief and grieving by children who *had* experienced a death in the family, then the ethical implications would both be much clearer and more available for mitigation. The ethical researcher must balance the potential benefit of the research with the potential emotional harm to the participant, and once again the question of informed consent becomes essential. On a procedural level most universities will have a more intensive ethical approval process if your research involves vulnerable participants whose vulnerable characteristic is also the substantive topic of the research.

Conversely vulnerable groups such as marginalized young people who are excluded from school may be in the position of being over-researched on an individual level, not in terms of academic research but in terms of having their movements, motives and behaviour surveilled and documented for a variety of purposes. Aaltonen (2017) explores the ethical issues surrounding working with such young people and in particular considers the question of negotiating and renegotiating informed consent when working with them longitudinally.

Dilemmas of being a teacher-researcher

Several researchers have highlighted that for teacher-researchers there are points at which researcher ethics and practitioner ethics may point to different courses of action (Cochran-Smith and Lytle 2009; Groundwater-Smith and Mockler 2007; Mockler 2014). One of the most troubling facts about researching your own practice or the practice of others in your own context is that you may have to find 'unwelcome truths' (Kemmis 2006); there are ethical as well as practical questions inherent in who your audience for the finished research will be. If the outcome of your research is that a key classroom questioning technique promoted by your Senior Leadership Team or Head teacher does not elicit the kind of complex thought it should, how are you going to present that information? If you include other teachers in your research then you must also think carefully about how you are going to represent them to others, no matter what the outcome of the research. Whether you make participants anonymous or not, the closer someone is to the research, the more likely they are to be able to identify who took part and who you are writing about.

Other dilemmas arise in the classroom. If you are intending to collect 'natural' data then you may begin second-guessing yourself as to whether you would be asking certain questions or acting in a certain way if the camera were not recording. If you are conducting an intervention and evaluating it using classroom discourse then you may be tempted not to stick to the plan if it seems to be going badly – in fact your professional ethics of responsibility to the students' learning may compel you to abandon your plan. Recording classroom discourse also brings up instances of children using inappropriate language (not just 'beer' as in case example 11.2 but swear words and pejorative terms). Value judgements made by external researchers are not necessarily accurate as they don't know the context; teachers' normal policing of language may be interrupted by being recorded.

Collection and Storage of data

One of the main ethical considerations is surprisingly practical: What data do you actually need to collect? We discuss the question of audio versus video in the next chapter, but there is an ethical dimension to that decision. You might also think about whether you need participants to generate extra data especially for your project or whether you can simply record naturally occurring data. While it is sometimes necessary to ask participants to do extra tasks in order to generate the right data to answer the research question, you also need to think about how much you are asking of them, particularly if they are children, and if it falls within what they might reasonably (or normally) be expected to do. A further issue arises as to when you ask students to complete tasks that you require for their participation. Are you asking them to give up break times or lunch times, for example, and if so, what proportion of their time is a reasonable amount to ask? You may find that if you are explicit (as you should be) in this requirement when you are recruiting participants then you get fewer students agreeing to take part. On the other hand, if you ask them to undertake tasks in lesson time when they must miss out on normal classwork there are also ethical implications regarding your effect on their educational progress.

Another question to ask yourself is how much data you need. There needs to be a balance between having enough to be able to answer your research question and having so much that you cannot use it or process it. Is it ethical to collect data if you will not use it? You may feel that if you are recording lessons that would be occurring anyway this is less of an issue than if you are asking students to write 3000-word essays on scientific knowledge.

An important ethical question is that of storage of data. When you have collected data, particularly involving recordings of children, it is very important to make sure it cannot be accessed by anyone not involved in the project. In general researchers in universities are required to keep audio and video recordings as password-protected files, and to only share them with those directly involved in the research project, via a secure internet transfer or on password-protected USB. Anonymized transcriptions can be treated a little less cautiously, but it is important that transcriptions do not carry identifying information about colleagues, students or even the school. If you have gained informed consent then you will have asked your participants to agree to their data being held for a certain amount of time; in general anonymised transcripts can be kept forever, but data with identifying marks needs to be destroyed.

If your data is the written work of pupils then make sure that the copies you keep do not have names or other identifying information in the text. Most university ethics requirements would require you to keep hard copies under lock and key but if you are an independent researcher you may feel other arrangements are more appropriate.

Publication/sharing of data

It is important to include some reference to publication and sharing of data in your gaining of consent from participants. Confidentiality is the usual requirement of publication and sharing. We have already mentioned the important issue relating to reporting research within your own school and the ease of identifying participants and laying them open to criticism. It is also worthwhile remembering that if you present research at larger venues, such as conferences or TeachMeets, you may have some of your participants in the audience. Victoria once presented her doctoral research at a large evening seminar sponsored by an educational charity and was questioned at the end by someone who it turned out had been involved in the study. It gave an important lesson in making sure you would be happy to have your participants hear how you have represented them! While twelve-year-olds are less likely to be in the audience at such events, you may find that when you write up your research they will go looking for it. Participants will be keen to identify themselves in your research. It is wise to remember Brooks and colleagues' (2014: 136) statement that 'scholars have a fundamental right to conduct research and publish their findings, limited only by the *overarching principles of harm prevention, respect and justice*' (our emphasis).

In education there is also an ethical imperative to disseminate research if you have found something that demonstrates common practice is problematic, or if you have found a better way to do something. It may have been the intention to improve your own teaching that started you on the research path, but if you have the power to improve the teaching of others, you are making more worthwhile the contribution of your participants.

If you have recorded video material and it is key to presenting your research, or conveying its message in public, then you need to think how that material might be best anonymized for public consumption. There are software which you can use to blur faces, or which provide line drawings to replace photographic images; it is a balancing act as to whether these remove essential data and negate the value of the video. A general rule is that there should be no direct identifiers, such as names, faces or logos visible.

Conclusion

Ethical research requires an ongoing attention to the potential for harm, seen in its broadest sense. There are rarely easy answers and classroom discourse can raise challenges in unexpected ways because it is unpredictable. Responding to participants ethically and understanding how that can affect your data is part of that challenge. We have mainly steered clear of discussing procedures in this chapter, instead choosing to focus on the kinds of ethical issues that might be raised by research in classroom discourse. It is up to the researcher to be thinking continually about the ethical implications of each decision they make, and it is important to remember that ethics is not something that you simply 'do' at the beginning of the research to get it out of the way: it permeates every stage of research design, data collection, analysis and dissemination.

Being a teacher-researcher offers particular ethical challenges because of the additional ethical responsibilities attached to being responsible for a group of children, and the competing needs of the two roles which you are inhabiting. For those without an institutional university affiliation, the onus is on the individual to think carefully about the ethics of their project. Action researchers may be particularly affected by this, as their research will tend to impact the learning of students directly, even if it is within the bounds of normal classroom practice. We would encourage you to talk through all the possible ethical implications with a critical friend or colleague, and to be as wide ranging and imaginative as possible in listing initial potential problems. You may then decide on mitigating practices or simply that the risk is so remote as to be irrelevant, but you are doing so from a position of knowledge rather than from assumption.

Further reading

American Educational Research Association (2011), Code of ethics, *Educational Researcher*, 40(3): 145–156. These are the national guidelines for educational researchers in the United States.

Australian Association for Research in Education (1993), *AARE Code of ethics*. Available at: https://www.aare.edu.au/research-and-advocacy/research-ethics/. These are the national guidelines for educational researchers in Australia.

British Educational Research Association (BERA) (2018), *Ethical guidelines for educational research* (4th edition). Available at: https://www.bera.ac.uk/wp-content/uploads/2018/06/BERA-Ethical-Guidelines-for-Educational-Research_4thEdn_2018.pdf. Similarly these are the national guidelines for educational researchers in the UK. Other national research associations will have their own guidelines.

Brooks, R., K.Te Riele and M. Maguire, (2014), *Ethics and education research*, London: SAGE. This book is a wide-ranging and comprehensive consideration of ethical problems, procedures and issues in education research. This is recommended for those who are particularly interested in ethics or have realized they have a specific ethical dilemma rather than the general reader.

CHAPTER TWELVE

Data Collection

Introduction

Collecting classroom discourse data in naturally occurring settings has a number of challenges associated with it. If you are lucky enough to work in a school which has an observation classroom with in-built recording facilities, then you will have far fewer practical problems. However, for everyone else naturally occurring discourse provides particular challenges for data generation. This chapter considers the different possibilities, practical issues like audibility and intrusiveness, and how data collection can be organized optimally for the particular focus of the research. Changes in the norms of research in this area have been created by advances in technology; we explore the advantages and challenges involved in using video cameras and computer-based technologies.

It is worth noting that the more correct phrase is 'data generation' in that by making the recording you are creating the data – without your intervention there would be no data. The more colloquial 'data collection', however, is widely used, and we have used both in this chapter.

Sampling

Generating data requires a number of considerations about who and what you are going to be working with. Some of these considerations are easy to ignore if you are studying your own practice, but we would encourage you to think carefully about things like, for example, choice of class or students, if they are doing group work.

If you are recording data from other people's classrooms, sampling will be affected by who you can recruit. You may want to consider that bias can be introduced into your data because you are likely to be easily able to record teachers who are confident in their practice. Teachers will also recommend you record their interactions with certain classes; it's likely to be easier to gain access to higher attaining classes, or 'nice' classes without behavioural challenges, for example. This may affect what you can claim from your data. It will also pose particular challenges if you are specifically looking at underrepresented or marginalized students (and gaining parental consent can also be more of a challenge with these students). You may find your position as an insider or an outsider will also affect what kind of access you can gain to classes; will you be more easily able to recruit teachers from your own school or outside your school? (This will likely relate to both issues of trust and what you are investigating.) If you are not a practising teacher, or have not been, then you may have to work harder to develop relationships with potential participants. There are a number of useful publications which talk about gaining access as an outsider, such as Walford (2001). 'Insider' status, either as a teacher in general or as a member of a specific school or subject community can also affect your ability to make sense of the data. On the other hand, it can lead you into making assumptions based on your background knowledge which are not necessarily upheld by the data (see Chapter 2 for further discussion of this).

When deciding who and what to record you may want to consider:

- Which age groups do you want to include? Does it matter if all classes are not the same age?

- Are the teachers you are studying specialists in their subject? How much experience do they have?

- If you are studying your own practice, do you need to find another teacher (or more) for consideration?

- Assuming you are working within a single subject, does the topic need to be the same (probability in mathematics, for example), or of the same type (a novel study in English, for example) for each class you are recording?

Sampling is also inherent in decisions you make about positioning of cameras and microphones (see discussion below).

Audibility

A key factor in the quality of classroom discourse data and in minimizing later frustration is the audibility of speakers in the recording. Classrooms are inherently noisy places and background noise can be problematic. In addition teachers and children usually face in different directions so it is difficult to pick up both sets of voices with the same microphone. In the absence of specialist facilities like those described in case example 12.1, compromises will always be made. One suggested approach is to have a microphone attached to the teacher, which will pick up their voice and anyone they speak one-on-one to during the lesson; the whole-class discussion can then be captured by the microphone attached to the video camera, providing it is positioned correctly. Traditional classrooms where turns are strictly controlled (Ingram and Elliott 2016) are likely to provide the most audible whole-class data, because there will be less background noise. (Note that there will not be none, because classrooms echo, have electric lights which hum and also many extraneous noises which are tuned out by your brain normally but which will become very clear in an audio recording.)

Case example 12.1:

International Centre for Classroom Research, located in the Melbourne Graduate School of Education at the University of Melbourne

Context: The International Centre for Classroom Research houses one of the largest collections of classroom data ever collected, initiated by the Learners' Perspective Study, which was a study of well-taught mathematics from across sixteen countries. They hold a data repository which includes data from mathematics and science classrooms across stages, medical education and tertiary settings.

Goal: To generate and provide a repository for classroom discourse data of high quality.

Outcomes: A wide range of studies are hosted or run by the Centre which illuminate classroom discourse in different disciplines and countries. Visit their website for further details (http://www.iccr.edu.au).

Methods: The Centre has a specially designed classroom which is built to maximize the quality of classroom discourse data which can be gathered. The classroom has ten cameras HD pan tilt zoom, wall and ceiling mounted; eight ceiling mounted microphones; one teacher platform microphone; and thirteen radio lapel mikes. The control room has sixteen channels of HD video capture and all videos are captured in sync via a custom software and available post lesson as a HD video file. There are thirty-two channels of audio capture. Teachers are invited to bring their normal classes in to the centre to teach in the classroom but there are also some experimental lessons taught in order to generate data for specific studies. The centre also has an observation room for small group work with four cameras, six lapel radio microphones and a one-way window.

If you are studying small group interactions you will need one recording per group. You may also need to reduce the naturalness of your data, in providing a quieter place for groups to talk – such as using breakout space if it is available in the context in which you are collecting data. Alternatively small group work may be better studied not in class, but in specific recording sessions, although this will also have implications for what you can claim from your data.

Audibility is also important for decisions about transcription; professional transcription services who do not have educational background knowledge will struggle more with less audible tape, but even with strong audibility are liable to misinterpret terms which an insider would hear (or rather interpret) accurately. When Jenni arranges for professional transcription she will ask for a transcriber with mathematics knowledge so they can pick up terms such as median instead of medium, for example. If you have a less audible recording you may prefer to use your own knowledge to supplement the transcription process. Many researchers take extensive notes while recording as a back up to enable them to interpret less audible data at a later point.

Do you need to be able to identify the speaker?

A key question which relates to the purpose of your study and what you are trying to find out is whether it is necessary or not for you to be able to attribute utterances to specific students in a class discussion. For some researchers who are only interested in teacher–student interaction, particularly in a CA context, student utterances need only to be categorized as 'student' so it is not necessary to be able to attribute them to specific people. However, in cases where student–student interaction is of interest, or where the development of an individual's utterances across a lesson is of interest, you will need to be able to identify them. It is difficult to do this from just audio recording; while the difference between adult and child is relatively easy to identify, the difference between different child voices is not. This is one of the advantages of using video data, in that there are visual cues as to who is speaking. If you cannot use video recording you may need to find some way of recording manually the order of speakers in important interactions, such as the use of a seating plan and written notes. If you are working with recordings of your own classroom you will also find it easier to identify who said what but this will mean transcribing your own data, and doing it as soon after the point of collection as possible in order to maximize your chances of accurate attribution while memory of the lesson can help you.

Intrusiveness

One of the problems is that children can react to the presence of a video camera or a microphone, particularly if it's a novel experience, or is accompanied by a stranger. This is exacerbated if you are also part of an intervention where there is a deliberate change in practice of what is being observed. You might have heard of a 'Hawthorne effect', which is a reference to a very old study which changed lighting conditions in a factory and found that productivity went up when lighting was improved – but then it also went up when lighting was lowered (Mayo 1949). A 'Hawthorne effect' therefore refers to the fact that simply being studied can create a desired change in behaviour which is not related to the intervention. Schuck and Kearney (2006) noted that some researchers actually instigate change, for example by asking classes to be quiet so as to reduce background noise and increase audibility of the speaker. This is a practical solution to the problem of audibility but it does not make for naturally occurring data.

You can try to reduce the intrusiveness of the data collection by careful positioning of cameras. Alternatively, researchers tend to find that children rapidly become accustomed to the change (Bogdan and Biklen 1998) so after a while they revert to 'normal' classroom behaviour. This might have implications for whether you use your initial data collection in your main data analysis, or if you decide to begin accustoming students to the presence of cameras and microphones before starting real data collection. You may also find that the 'YouTube generation' is not as affected by the presence of cameras in its classroom!

How much data do you need or want?

It is very easy to collect too much data: Martin-Beltrán (2010) collected 300 hours of classroom audio data, which is far more than most of us want to sift through! It is important to think carefully about how much data you need in order to fulfil the aims of your research. The amount you will need to record can also differ depending on the kind of research you are doing. There is a difference, for example, between studies of naturally occurring data and experimental interventions – you need to collect more of the first in order to get enough examples of a specific item of interest, such as explanations. When Jenni was investigating what interactional structures lead to student explanations without the teacher explicitly asking for them she analysed forty-one hours of mathematics whole-class interactions; one type of structure, where the teacher generated an argument between students, resulted in an explanation just seven times in the whole data set (reported in Ingram et al. 2018). Jenni generally spends an hour per hour of data to listen to it to identify parts of the lesson that will be of interest, before she begins the time required for transcription or close analysis.

Many close linguistic approaches do not depend on quantity of data but on quality, so having extra hours of data is only useful if they illuminate the problem further in some way. Depending on the study you are conducting you may want to carry out some analysis before deciding if you need further data recording of a specific year group, or of a specific part of a lesson, for example.

The focus of research and optimal data generation

A more important question than how much data is what data you want to collect, and what is the best data for answering your particular research question. One approach is to do an initial data collection to see what areas of interest spring up and then to do a more targeted data generation phase – for example if after recording a few lessons with a Year 9 history group it becomes clear that the most important and interesting classroom discussion for your purposes happens during the introduction to the lesson then you could focus on recording just the first twenty minutes of more lessons, rather than spending time recording, for example, intensive writing, which does not give you any more useful data.

Video cameras and computer-based technologies

Video cameras have become the norm for classroom discourse data collection over the last decade, mostly because of the ease of attributing utterances to individuals and being able to see contextual information such as what the teacher is writing on the whiteboard.

While video recording can produce extremely rich data for research in classroom discourse, the use of video cameras entails making a number of choices every time you use them in the classroom, such as position, frame, angle and closeness to the action (Fitzgerald et al. 2013). These choices will dictate what you can and cannot see from the final recording. Fitzgerald, Hackling and Dawson, for example, recommend that zooming is kept to a minimum during recording, because the risk of missing something important during the zoom in or out is too high when balanced against the gains of the close zoom in.

Some researchers, particularly teachers recording their own practice, have found the use of tablet computers to record video to be convenient and easily available. They can mostly be positioned flexibly in the classroom, and are unobtrusive and familiar sights. They also have the advantage of easy data storage and transfer.

If you are interested in non-verbal communication, such as eye gaze, body posture, facial expressions or gestures, then you will need video recording from different angles in order to capture these. You may need to work with smaller groups in order to make this practicable.

Collecting interview data

After the complexities of recording naturally occurring classroom discourse, generating interview data is a walk in the park. A single microphone usually suffices, and digital voice recorders are fine for the purpose. It is still important to consider background noise, particularly in school, as smaller rooms which are used for interviews are often in noisier parts of the school which may have doors banging, for example. Other things to consider are bells and lesson changeover: you may be able to hear the person you are interviewing but the tape will pick up corridor noise as clearly as the voice data.

When interviewing students you will want to consider the pros and cons of interviewing individuals versus small groups. Having more than one student can enable them to open up and be more likely to talk; you can gain valuable data when students disagree with one another and talk about a topic on tape. On the other hand, the individual relationships involved are critical in relation to this: if one student is dominant then the other may defer to their views; if they are not friends then they may be less responsive than if they were alone. If only one is from a marginalized group (including lower attainers) then they may be less willing to speak about their experiences that do not reflect those of the other student, whereas having a pair of them with similar backgrounds may enable them to open more to you.

This raises a further issue if you are a teacher interviewing students, and particularly if you are interviewing students whom you teach. The ways in which we speak as teachers to student are not necessarily productive in interviewing and can introduce systematic bias into data collection. Write an interview schedule (list of questions) beforehand and ask someone else to read it over to check for leading questions. Interviewers should be careful to be neutrally encouraging, and silence makes a useful tool for getting interviewees to continue talking rather than stopping at a pause (just as it does in getting students to extend their answers in class) (Kvale 2008).

Textual data collection

For textual data analysis (see Chapter 10), data collection can be very simple. Some data sets such as class essays or school policies are easily delineated and therefore clear cut to assemble. For others, such as studies looking at government policies, where the limits are less defined (only policy statements? Political speeches from policymakers? Op-ed columns in newspapers from policymakers?), both the decision-making process as to what to include and the practical process of finding the documents can be more complicated. Caveats as to the exhaustiveness of the search process may be part of the recorded methods in such studies.

Some written texts, and in particular multimodal texts, can be in the form of artefacts: physical objects which need to be stored. There may also be digital artefacts associated with a study of classroom discourse, such as photographs of what teachers' have written on the whiteboard. Case example 12.2 describes a study which used physical artefacts as a key part of the data generation process and an article which reflects on their use. The use of photographs generated some particular ethical issues for the researchers in analysis and sharing of data.

Case example 12.2:

'Producing different knowledge and producing knowledge differently': Rethinking physical education research and practice through participatory visual methods (Enright and O'Sullivan 2012)

Context: A three-year Participatory Action Research project in Ireland with forty-one teenage girls associated with a disadvantaged urban school.

Goal: To critique the use of two participatory methods using artefacts: photovoice and timelines.

Outcomes: The article suggests that participatory methods work best in the context of a range of methods, and when they align with the fundamental aim of the research. The use of different participatory methods enabled the researchers to uncover contradictions in their data; participants reflected that an initial diary exercise had produced inaccurate data because they had inflated the amount of physical activity they engaged in, believing that was what the researchers wanted them to say. Asking students to engage in analysis meant that they interpreted and reinterpreted the data, shifting between interpretations of the photographs and timelines. The researchers also reflected on the problematic ethics of asking young people to take photographs as data, given the potential for those pictures to show people who were unaware they were being photographed, or who were identifiable, or to show harmful activities. Some photographs were held back from group discussion because of the way they represented participants.

Methods: The study asked participants in the main study to reflect on their use of the participatory methods. Participatory methods are ones which facilitate the ability of participants to articulate what they know and which give them more control over the research process. Photovoice is a method where participants are asked to take photos of their lives in relation to the topic of interest (in this case topics like 'my physically active life') and then the photos are used as the focus for individual or group discussion, which therefore in theory derives from the parts of their lives which participants wish to highlight. Timelines are a method where participants are asked to indicate on a timeline critical incidents in their lives (in this case of relevance to their engagement in physical activity). They can use both written and pictorial representations to create meaning. This study then invited participants to be part of inductive analysis workshops where they reflected on the use of these methods, and the audio recordings of those workshops were used as the data for this chapter. The researchers approached this from a feminist perspective, aiming to give their participants more control over the research process and to engage their participants in an ongoing dialogue.

Photoelicitation can be a useful tool for generating interesting data on classrooms, students, and teaching and learning (Harper 2002). You may also wish to consider combining records of classroom interaction such as videos with 'stimulated recall 'interviews (see Nind et al. 2016 for more on this technique) where short extracts of the recording are shown to the teacher (usually) and they are asked to talk about the area of interest in relation to that extract (see Haw and Hadfield [2011] for a full account of this and other uses of video in social science research).

Artefacts can present particular challenges for the data analysis period of a research study. Software used for qualitative data analysis allows you to import photographs, video, audio and jpegs and to code them as if they were written data. This may be a suitable approach for you. Whether using software or analysing 'by hand' you will need to think carefully about how artefacts relate to other sources of data and how that relationship can be preserved in the data analysis process and the eventual write up.

Data management – file names and labelling, archiving and open access

Clarity is essential in dealing with the labelling of data. It is useful to think out in advance how you are going to label and file data (whether physically or in digital form), particularly if you are going to generate a lot of data. Having a system set up beforehand can save a lot of time later; we have lost count of the number of research projects where we have had to reorganize (or just organize!) data into a more useful and usable configuration. You will also need to take into account data protection regulations in your country if you have data which carries identifying information about individuals and their characteristics.

If you are recording classroom interactions you may want to store data grouped by the teacher (use a pseudonym) or by the year groups, or by the subject – depending on the range of data which you are collecting and the purpose of your study. If you want to be able to match data from different time points collected at the same location or from the same person you will need a key to make sure that you can identify 'school 1' or 'Simon the teacher' when six months or a year has passed. This key to pseudonyms is a document which must remain password protected for ethical and legal reasons, and kept separate from the data.

Data sharing and archiving is becoming increasingly common. Sharing your data enables other researchers to validate your own research, but also offers the opportunities for them to broaden or generalize your findings, or to build new theories. You will need to consider, when, who and how to share your data at the earliest stages of your research as it will often form part of your consent procedures. Generally, you should only share finalized and anonymized data. Many institutions and journals now offer facilities for data sharing and data archiving, but to be useful to other researchers you will need to ensure you can include the relevant meta data about your participants and the data collected. Data needs to be shared in a way that enables other researchers to make sense of the data itself, rather than your analysis of it as in other publications.

There are also decisions around data analysis that need considering at the outset of your research. These include decisions around transcription which we consider in the next chapter, but also decisions about whether to, how to and what to code. The analysis stage often involves some sort of data reduction which Miles and Huberman (1994) describe as 'the process of selecting, focusing, simplifying, abstracting, and transforming the data that appear in written up field notes or transcriptions' (p. 10). The most common coding practices include 'structural coding' or open coding which are usually predetermined to match your interview questions or categories identified in the literature, 'selective coding' which focuses on codes that will enable you to specifically address the hypotheses embedded in your research questions, and 'axial coding' which involves adding dimensions to your existing codes, for example high or low for degree of confidence or the number of times a student asks a question. The decisions around coding will depend upon your theoretical and methodological approach but a useful guide can be found in Saldana (2015).

Conclusion

We have considered a number of the practical issues which are important to consider when setting out to generate classroom data. However, the complexities of what happens when you actually start collecting data could be a field of literature in its own right. Researchers often share confessional tales of the realities of research which are not recorded in their official accounts of the research process, but which are illustrative of the potential pitfalls. The Twitter hashtag #HonestMethods can provide some illumination in this matter.

One of the topics we have not covered in this book in detail is a more general look at data analysis other than the specifics we have considered in relation to each theoretical and methodological approach in Part One. Some further reading is given below or see Elliott (2018) for an account of questions to ask when undertaking qualitative data coding. Data analysis takes a lot longer than data collection but this is often overlooked in the planning stage. One of the issues we have highlighted in this chapter is the need for careful preparation to ensure that the quality of data you generate is both good enough for your purpose and organized enough for ease of analysis. It is easy to rush into data collection without thinking through potential difficulties and this can prevent your being able to make the claims you want at the end of the process.

Further Reading

Heath, C., J. Hindmarsh and P. Luff (2010), *Video in qualitative research*, London: Sage. A comprehensive account of the use of video as a data generation method.

Kvale, S. (2008), *Doing interviews*, London: Sage. This is the classic text on conducting interviews and considers all issues including the writing of interview schedules and interpersonal behaviour during data collection.

Miles, M.B., A.M. Huberman and J. Saldana (2013), *Qualitative data analysis*, London: Sage. This is another classic text (regularly updated) on the analysis of qualitative data which provide a detailed and practical guide for general approaches to data analysis.

CHAPTER THIRTEEN

Transcription Decisions

Introduction

Many researchers dive straight into transcribing before thinking about the decisions they need to make before they start, or even whether they need to transcribe at all. Transcription is not theory-neutral or objective: it needs to match your research aims and methodology. A 'transcript is a text that "re"-presents an event; it is not the event itself' (Green et al. 1997: 172). Transcriptions need to be constructed so that they are useful for your analysis, but not overwhelming. In other words, they should only include the details you need for your analysis. Transcripts range from researchers writing a sense of what participants said, to detailed annotated transcripts including a wide range of paralinguistic features, but these different transcripts serve different purposes and it is the purpose of the transcript that should drive the nature and content of what you transcribe.

Transcripts are only ever partial representations of the data collected, they are instead tools which can help you analyse and understand the data you have collected. They necessarily reduce the video or audio data you have collected. Therefore, transcription is part of the analysis of your data, not part of data collection.

Making decisions about transcription

Do you need to transcribe? Researchers often assume that they need to transcribe their data as that is how most researchers work with data. However, the range of software available to support you in your research now enables you to directly code audio and video files without necessarily transcribing. If, for example, you have a predetermined coding framework that you are applying to your data, then you can code the audio or video file just as easily as you could code a transcript.

So, it is worth spending time thinking about why you are transcribing and what it is that you are transcribing. For example, in case example 13.1 the researchers only transcribed specific instances they were interested in within their data, and not all of their interactional data. If you choose to code the data directly, you can always transcribe the short sections you need to share through your writing or at conference presentations.

Case example 13.1:

Positioning students as readers and writers through talk in a high school English classroom (Vetter 2010)

Context: A five-month study of an English teacher's eleventh-grade classroom in the United States focusing on the teacher's improvised responses during literacy teaching.

Goal: To examine how the teacher used responses to students' utterances to position them as members of a writing community who were capable writers and engaged readers. The goal is to provide models of successful interactions for other teachers and teacher educators.

Outcomes: The article uses detailed analysis of three 'literacy events', conducted through the lens of positioning theory, to show how the teacher successfully used improvised interactions to position students positively in relation to reading and writing. The author analyses episodes to show the teacher moving students from disengaged to engaged, to successful literacy learners, through various methods in improvised interactions. For example, appropriating put-downs by the pupils to position them as part of a reading community, rather than shutting them down. This gave the students independence and agency within a literacy event. Similarly, she positioned herself as a facilitator rather than a director. Through detailed analysis of the content of teacher–student interactions the author demonstrates how students adopt the identities they are positioned into by the teacher, for better (in this case) or for worse. The author concludes that teachers need to be sophisticated users of improvised interactions in the classroom.

Methods: The study used a micro-ethnographic approach, using discourse analysis framed around positioning theory. The researcher was a participant-observer, collecting data that included expanded field notes, video and audio recordings of classroom interactions, and interviews with the teacher and the twenty-five students in her eleventh-grade English class. Between three and five fifty-minute classes a week were observed over five months. Recordings and field notes were examined for examples of how the teacher used language to position students as readers/writers, and for counter examples for students being alienated from literacy events. Cleaned up transcriptions of episodes of interest were made to evidence claims. Discourse analysis focused on how the teacher shaped students' positions. Claims were checked with other researchers and member checking was carried out with students and the teacher. Transcription was simple verbatim but include some discourse features such as laughter that were relevant to the positioning theory approach to analysis. Only parts of the video and audio recordings of the lessons that were considered pertinent were transcribed. The interviews with the class teacher were not transcribed.

Some aspects of interaction are also notoriously difficult to transcribe such as bodily movements and gestures, and when you are particularly interested in these features and when you want to remain close to the interaction in your analysis, working with the video files directly might be more effective. If you intend to do any form of quantitative analysis, such as corpus linguistics as we describe in Chapter 6, then you are likely to need to transcribe the entirety of your collected data but often only the words used without any features of prosody etc. is needed. A mixed-methods approach may require you to transcribe in two different ways: one that can be read by computer software for the quantitative analysis and a more detailed transcript for the qualitative analysis.

There are also reasons why you might want to work solely with transcripts in your analysis. Working with transcripts puts limits on the data you are working with which can help you to focus specifically on what you are interested in without being distracted by other features. If you are only interested in the content of what participants are saying, then you may prefer to work exclusively with transcripts. One disadvantage to working exclusively with transcripts in your analysis is that you can lose sight of the original data. Continuing to work with the audio and video data helps you to stay familiar with your data as you analyse it. Many researchers using CA frequently re-transcribe their data as this enables them not only to stay close to the recorded data, but also to see or hear different features of the interaction as the analysis progresses. You may also find that you need to produce different transcriptions at different times during the analysis in order to examine different aspects of the data being transcribed as your ideas and foci change over time.

One of the key decisions you will need to make once you have decided that you will be transcribing is what to include in the transcript. This is accompanied by the equally important decision of what to ignore. One of the important questions to consider is whether you are solely interested in *what* your participants are saying or whether you are also interested in *how* they are saying it. The answer to this question will also then lead to whether you need to use a specific transcription convention.

Compare the two transcripts offered below taken from a transcript of a video of a maths lesson that Jenni collected as part of her research. Transcript one just includes the words spoken by the teacher and the student. This representation of the interaction is easy to read and enables you to focus on what is being said.

Teacher: what did you do next?
Student: I did two times sixteen
Teacher: yeah
Student: then four times eight

TRANSCRIPT 13.1 *Verbatim transcript.*

The second transcription of the same interaction has made use of the Jefferson transcription system (2004), which is used extensively within Conversation Analytic research discussed in Chapter 2 and in case example 13.3, but it is also used within many other methodological approaches to the analysis of classroom interaction. This transcript is not as easy to read and is full of symbols indicating changes in pace (< and >), changes in pitch (↑ and ↓) as well as many other features of how the words were spoken such as the elongation of sounds (denoted by:), the length of pauses (denoted by the numbers in brackets, measured in seconds) and emphasis (the use of capital letters). The transcript also includes changes in punctuation, for example the question mark that appears at the end of the first line of the first transcript that is not included in the second transcript as in Jefferson notation punctuation indicates intonation, whereas in verbatim transcripts it usually serves to make the transcript more readable.

```
1 Teacher:  >↑what=d'a do< next
2           (0.8)
3 Student:  e:::r I (1.8) did ↑two (1.6) ti:::mes::
            (7.7) two
4           ti:mes: (2.4) six↑tee:n
5           (0.4)
6 Teacher:  >yeah.<
7           (4.4)
8 Student:  then ↓FO:ur times ↑eight
```

TRANSCRIPT 13.2 *Jefferson notation (see end of chapter for transcript notation).*

Notice also that the second transcript includes line numbers. This is an easy way to point to specific parts of a transcript in your analysis. You could also number the turns. Line numbers are an artefact of

Case example 13.2:

'Reading All that White Crazy Stuff:' Black young women unpacking whiteness in a high school British Literature classroom (Carter 2007)

Context: A case of a single literature lesson analysed using sociolinguistic analysis and black feminist theory. The lesson was part of a compulsory course on British Literature (in the United States) which the author observed two to three times a week over five months, of nineteen students of varying racial backgrounds including only two black female students. The lesson in question explored the text of Shakespeare's Sonnet 130 'My mistress' eyes are nothing like the sun'.

Goal: To examine how whiteness functions within the British Literature classroom (in the United States) and how interactions around the curriculum can negatively position black female students. The article uses a 'telling case' of one particular lesson to exemplify the potential for marginalization by the curriculum and to explore an issue of great importance to teachers and teacher educators.

Outcomes: The author demonstrates the exclusion of the black female students from the curriculum by a micro-analysis of the discussion, which centres around the question of female beauty in Sonnet 130. The concept of beauty in the poem is an exclusively white Eurocentric one, and the discussion reflects that, further marginalizing the black female students. The analysis demonstrates the tensions created for the two black female students by the way this topic is treated, their attempts to resist it and how it affects their participation in class. The students affirmed their resistance to and feelings of marginalization by the whiteness of the British Literature curriculum in a later interview.

Methods: The study uses a sociolinguistic ethnographic approach framed through black feminist theory. A classroom event – a discussion of Sonnet 130 – is transcribed verbatim but without paralinguistic features. The transcript is presented alongside an analysis of the points at which race becomes 'visible' within the interactions. Triangulation is provided by an interview with the two black female students, which is also transcribed verbatim, reflecting their linguistic patterning. This gives a voice to the students, a key concern of black feminist theoretical approaches.

the transcription, whereas turn numbers relate more closely to the structure of the interaction itself.

Case examples 13.1 and 13.2 illustrate the choice of whether to transcribe all of your data, and if not, what to transcribe. Both studies used triangulation through interviews with some of the participants and transcription is often needed for this, as it is a convenient way to share data with others. Case example 13.3 illustrates the use of a more detailed and complex transcript, which the analysis relies on heavily, but produces a transcript that is difficult to read and that is

Case example 13.3:

Learning to estimate in the mathematics classroom: A conversation-analytic approach (Forrester and Pike 1998)

Context: A study of two estimation lessons with pupils aged nine to eleven years old focusing on teachers' instructions and pupils' talk during small-group follow-up activities.

Goal: To examine how teachers and pupils orient to, and understand, measurement estimation as both a practical activity and a mathematical object. Specifically how the teachers and pupils learn to estimate in the classroom, including uncovering the implicit ideas embedded within the discourse around estimation tasks and activities. The authors identify four issues they examined through their analysis of the classroom interaction: the discourse surrounding estimation and measurement, the change in relationships between estimation and measurement over a lesson, the criteria used for judging the appropriateness of an estimation and evidence of conceptual understanding.

Outcomes: Through analysing the discourse of the teachers and the pupils the authors showed that estimation was understood by the students as associated with vagueness, ambiguity and guessing as well as not using a ruler. In contrast, measurement was associated with talk about correctness, the right answer and using a ruler. The fine-grained analysis of the transcript also enabled the authors to show how the meaning of what-it-is-to-estimate and what-it-is-to-measure evolved over the interaction, but also that in practice estimation was a practical activity and there was no evidence in the transcripts that the students had any conceptual understanding of estimation.

Methods: The study used ethnomethodologically informed conversation analysis. Six lessons on estimation were video recorded, three from each teacher, and were transcribed using what is now known as Jefferson Transcription (Psathas 1995). Both researchers independently transcribed the videos and then compared and resolved any differences. The analysis focused on the sequential structures of interactions that were co-constructed by the teacher and the pupils, including the sequential placement of the words measurement and estimation within the interaction. The researchers also used pausing, emphasis, volume, stretching and changes in pitch to identify how different words related to estimation and measurement were used and to mark out words that were being used as 'distinct discursive objects'. The researchers were able to uncover implicit metaphors and models used by the two teachers when talking about estimation and measurement.

not appropriate to share with participants without the experience of reading transcripts like this.

One reason why researchers using the ethnomethodological approaches discussed in Chapter 2 share such detailed transcripts is to enable the reader to see in the data the evidence for the claims and interpretations being made. Thus for these approaches it is important to publish the detailed transcript alongside the analysis as in case example 13.3. The other approaches used by case examples 13.1 and 13.2 have triangulated their data through a membership check which is a common way of validating the analysis within sociolinguistic approaches.

Transcribing non-verbal features of interaction

There are also now a range of transcription systems for dealing with non-verbal elements of interactions, such as eye gaze or specific gestures. Case example 13.4 is one well-known example of this by Charles Goodwin who is often described as the first researcher to treat non-verbal information systematically. The transcription of gestures and eye gaze can result in a very complex and detailed transcript, which is both difficult to read and also only partially represents what is going on. Many researchers now include photographs or line drawings (which preserve anonymity) as Goodwin does in case example 13.4. Each of these systems is still a static representation of the interaction. Many publishers now have

Case example 13.4:

Action and embodiment within situated human interaction (Goodwin 2000)

Context: This study draws upon two sources of data, but we focus here on his analysis of three girls playing hopscotch.

Goal: To examine how different semiotic resources are used simultaneously in interaction. In particular Goodwin treats both language and gesture as generating the context.

Outcomes: Goodwin's analysis brings together the talk-in-interaction and the bodily movements of the girls both to illustrate the differences between talk in communication and gestures in communication, and how the girls attend to this talk, the graphical representations and gestures to make sense of the situation. He shows how people's actions are made visible through multiple semiotic fields, not just language. In particular, he shows how many of the key ideas of CA, such as sequential organization and the situatedness of all interactions, apply to other semiotic fields and not just talk.

Methods: The girls were video recorded and these videos were transcribed. The transcriptions presented in the paper include diagrams of how the participants had been interacting with the physical environment of the game, and an English translation of what they were saying, and diagrams of the hand gestures one of the girls was using. The approach Goodwin takes is based on CA but with a focus on the multimodal actions rather than more specific features of talk, such as emphasis and pauses.

options to include videos online to accompany their publications which gives the reader a much fuller sense of the data and represents the dynamic nature of many gestures and interactions, but you need to take care to preserve the anonymity of your participants.

Since Goodwin's work a range of models for multimodal transcription have been developed. Many of these methods are summarized in Nind, Curtin and Hall's (2016: 196–197) chapter on pedagogy embodied in Table 8.1 as well as how these methods allow you to consider the various modes in which teachers and students communicate.

Translation

The translation of data is often needed if your audience may not necessarily be able to read the data directly themselves. In many cases this will not cause too many difficulties, but if the precise use of words, or overlapping speech and pausing are of interest than the different structures of the languages used means that an analysis of the original data would differ from an analysis of the translated data. Where this is the case most researchers include both the original transcript and the translation. However, there are still decisions that need to be made about how to present both representations. You could represent your data in two columns with the original transcription on one side and the translation on the other, but this will not work if the lines are long or if you are interested in overlapping speech. You could include the original transcript as a footnote or endnote which gives your reader access to it without distracting the reading of the translation, or you could use separate lines for each language. These decisions all have implications for how you are positioning each language in relation to each other.

Further practical considerations

Transcription can be very time-consuming, particularly if you need to include a wide range of features. For an hour's worth of interview data it can take around two hours to transcribe verbatim, but more like twelve hours for full Jefferson transcription. Most transcribers focus on one feature at a time, transcribing words first and then adding detail such as intonation or pauses with each pass. If you are new to transcription, new to the transcription style or new to the software you are using these times can be considerably longer. The time it takes to transcribe data is also affected by the equipment you are using, the quality of the recordings and the software you are using as well as your own expertise, including your typing speed.

There is now a wide range of software available to support you with your transcription. Your choice of software depends upon the kind of analysis you want to do. It is worth checking what software is available before you begin transcribe, as what is available is constantly changing and improving. For many purposes a standard word processing package will be sufficient. There are also some very sophisticated qualitative software packages that will enable you to align your transcripts to your audio or video files so you can quickly move to different sections of your data as you analyse it. This software often allows you to integrate multiple video recordings from different angles and audio recordings of the same event so you can move quickly between different viewpoints. These packages also enable you to code your data and many are compatible with transcription pedals if you want to use them. However, many of these packages can be expensive if your institution does not already have a licence.

NVivo (https://www.qsrinternational.com/nvivo/nvivo-products) and ATLAS.ti (atlasti.com) are widely available in many universities and have lots of support available to show you how to use it, but they are more suited to the coding the data rather than transcribing directly into the software itself and can require quite a lot of computer power for it to run smoothly with large data sets. It is definitely worth backing up regularly when you use these types of software. Transana (www.transana.com) is often a more affordable option and is our preferred choice for when we are transcribing using Jefferson because all the special characters are available as keyboard shortcuts and because of the way it works with the data it doesn't slow the computer down too much. However for verbatim transcribing we generally use a word processing package.

If you are looking to transcribe specific linguistic features, then there are also freely available software packages that can help you. Audacity (audacity.sourceforge.net) is a free piece of software designed to allow you to edit audio files, but also enable you to more accurately time pauses and can help you to clean up data that can be difficult to hear on the original recording. It also can be used to anonymize your audio files when you want to share them at conferences as you can record over names and change the voices of the speakers so they are less recognizable. If you are particularly interested in the prosody of the interactions then Praat (www.praat.org) is widely used to examine the pitch of what is being said. You may of course want to combine these software packages and use them for different purpose. For example, you can export transcripts from Transana and then import them into Nvivo or concordance tools such as AntConc (Anthony 2018).

While current voice recognition software is not reliable enough to do your transcription for you, it can speed up the process if you listen to your data while speaking to your voice recognition software. Of course this will only work for verbatim transcriptions and the researcher needs to be aware of the errors that can creep in doing it this way, particularly around technical language. For example, voice recognition is not very accurate in transcribing conversations about mathematics with median being recognized as medium, and equations needing careful transcription by hand. These types of errors are also common if you use a professional transcription service and it is always worth asking if they can use a transcriber who might be familiar with the context in which you collected your data. While using a professional transcription service will speed up the process of transcription, doing it yourself enables you to become more and more familiar with your data and to notice features that might be analytically of interest.

Conclusion

In this chapter we have presented transcription as a decision-making process. The term 'process' is also relevant in that transcription is rarely 'finished' as each time you watch or listen to your data you will notice new features. Many researchers do not consider what or how they are going to transcribe. We have seen many a student spend hours and hours transcribing all the data they have without considering first whether they needed to. On numerous occasions this has also led to less time being available for the actual analysis of the data, which is often the most interesting and most time-consuming part of research.

Jefferson Transcription Notation (from Sidnell 2010)

Convention	Name	Use
[text]	Brackets	Indicates the start and end points of overlapping speech.
(0.5)	Timed silence	Indicates the length, in seconds, of a silence.
(.)	Micropause	A hearable pause, usually less than 0.2 seconds.
.	Period	Indicates falling pitch or intonation.
? or ↑	Question mark or Up arrow	Indicates rising pitch or intonation.
,	Comma	Indicates a temporary rise or fall in intonation.

Table (*Continued*)

Convention	Name	Use
-	Hyphen	Indicates an abrupt halt or interruption in utterance.
°	Degree symbol	Indicates quiet speech.
underline	Underlined text	Indicates the speaker is emphasizing or stressing the speech.
:::	Colon(s)	Indicates prolongation of a sound.
(text)	Parentheses	Speech which is unclear in the transcript.

When thinking about the decisions you need to make around whether to transcribe, what to transcribe or how to describe reflect on how your own beliefs and ideologies are affecting these decisions. It is worth talking through these decisions with other researchers as your choices will influence how your data are read by others, possibly unintentionally emphasizing some speakers over others or some aspects of interaction over others.

Further Reading

Davidson, C. (2009), 'Transcription: Imperatives for qualitative research', *International Journal of Qualitative Methods*, 8 (2): 36–52. This paper offers a comprehensive review of literature on transcription and summarizes the issues raised by this literature as well as raising some interesting questions to consider.
Edwards, J.A. and M.D. Lampert (1993), *Talking data: Transcription and coding in discourse research*, Hillsdale, NJ and London: Erlbaum. This book details a range of models of transcription, linked to a range of theoretical perspectives, mostly from linguistics.

CHAPTER FOURTEEN

Conclusion

In this book we set out to introduce a range of ideas, concepts, and theoretical and methodological approaches that may be of use to the researcher interested in classroom discourse. Our goal was to raise awareness of the choices and decisions involved from the very beginning of conceptualizing and conducting research in this area, and to consider the implications that these decisions may have for your research design, your methods and for the claims which you can make from your research. We have used a range of studies from across sectors, cultures and contexts to exemplify and illuminate the different approaches possible and the vast array of studies that are conducted under the umbrella of classroom discourse research. We hope that the way we have presented and explored the issues and studies in this book will enable readers to reflect on their own thinking, preconceptions, unconscious decisions and interests. By examining such contrasting approaches we hope that we have broadened and deepened readers' awareness of the options available.

The challenge from the outset was the sheer diversity of approaches and the variability within approaches, even as regards something as simple as the meaning of the word 'discourse'. This has made accounts of some aspects necessarily sparse and we apologize for areas where the reader would have liked a fuller account. Some of these areas are those which have deeply felt social controversies attached to them (such as African American Vernacular English or the case for culturally differentiated epistemologies) and these could be (and are) entire books in themselves for those who are interested.

Although we have skated over the surface of these controversies, we have signposted them and we would urge anyone interested in working in those areas to do substantial further reading. We have shown in Chapter 7 the integral relationship between language and identity, the implication of which is that there is always the potential for controversy in researching linguistic matters, and therefore the potential for emotional harm to the participant. Or, in the terminology we considered in Chapter 5, the potential for results to be face-threatening, whether for participants, researchers and recipients of the research. In Chapter 11 we discussed the ethical implications of this, and the responsibility of the researcher to prevent harm, among many other provocations to ethical thought.

Addressing both theoretical and practical considerations within the same text is a challenge in its own right, yet one which we feel strongly not enough research methods texts rise to. We hope the mix of practical advice found in Chapters 11, 12 and 13, together with our consideration of practical implications throughout the rest of the book offers this to the reader, but also that we have offered pointers of where to go to find out more. Part Two selected just a few of the applications that can be made of the different theoretical perspectives considered in Part One; some of these are challenges globally to the educator no matter what sector they find themselves in, such as the nature of knowledge (Chapter 9) or multilingual classrooms (Chapter 8).

We have characterized language, both written and spoken, throughout the book as being socially constructed, and the result of choices which have been made by writers and speakers, implicitly or explicitly, consciously or not. Some of the approaches we have discussed in this book seek specifically to make these choices in construction tangible while others treat them as a given.

The approaches we have covered in the book include both long-established fields, such as CA (Chapter 2), and others which are relative newcomers and still evolving, where you might make a contribution to the methodology of the field, such as translanguaging (Chapter 8), or pedagogies associated with research findings. In writing the book we have come across applications of theories to topics which we had not expected, and have ourselves come up with new ideas for research studies. In the end, this is the best we hope for from this book for any reader or for ourselves from its writing: to learn new things and to provoke new thinking.

REFERENCES

Aaltonen, S. (2017), Challenges in gaining and re-gaining informed consent among young people on the margins of education, *International Journal of Social Research Methodology*, 20 (4): 329–341.

Alexander, R. (2018). Developing dialogic teaching: Genesis, process, trial, *Research Papers in Education*, 33 (5): 561–598.

American Educational Research Association (2011), Code of ethics, *Educational Researcher*, 40 (3): 145–156.

Anderson, K. T. (2009), Applying positioning theory to the analysis of classroom interactions: Mediating micro-identities, macro-kinds, and ideologies of knowing, *Linguistics and Education*, 20 (4): 291–310. https://doi.org/10.1016/j.linged.2009.08.001.

Anderson, K. T. and S. J. Zuiker (2010), Performative identity as a resource for classroom participation: Scientific Shane vs. Jimmy Neutron, *Journal of Language, Identity and Education*, 9 (5): 291–309. https://doi.org/10.1080/15348458.2010.517708.

Antaki, C. and S. Widdicombe (1998), *Identities in talk*, London: Sage.

Antaki, C., M. G. Billig, D. Edwards and J. A. Potter (2003), Discourse analysis means doing analysis: A critique of six analytic shortcomings, *Discourse Analysis Online*, 1. http://extra.shu.ac.uk/daol/articles/v1/n1/a1/antaki2002002.html.

Anthony, L. (2018), *AntConc*, Tokyo: Waseda University.

Arnold, J. (2012), Science students' classroom discourse: Tasha's umwelt, *Research in Science Education*, 42 (2): 233–259. https://doi.org/10.1007/s11165-010-9195-0.

Arribas-Ayllon, M. and V. Walkerdine (2008), 'Foucauldian discourse analysis', in C. Willig and W. Stainton-Rogers (eds), *The SAGE handbook of qualitative research in psychology*, 91–109, London: Sage.

Atkinson, P. and A. Coffey (2010), 'Analysing documentary realities', in D. Silverman (ed.), *Qualitative research* (3rd edn), London: Sage.

Atwood, S., W. Turnbull and J. I. M. Carpendale (2010), The construction of knowledge in classroom talk, *Journal of the Learning Sciences*, 19 (3): 358–402. DOI: 10.1080/10508406.2010.481013.

Australian Association for Research in Education (1993), *AARE Code of ethics*. Available at: https://www.aare.edu.au/research-and-advocacy/research-ethics/.

Baker, C. (2011), *Foundations of bilingual education and bilingualism*, Clevedon: Multilingual Matters.

Baker, C. and A. Sienkewicz (2000), *The care and education of young bilinguals*, Clevedon: Multilingual Matters.

Baker, P. (2006), *Using corpora in discourse analysis*, London: Continuum.

Barlow, M. (2002), *MonoConcPro*, Houston, TX: Athelstan.

Barnard, C. (2003), 'Pearl Harbor in Japanese high school history textbooks', in J. R Martin and R. Wodak (eds), *Re/reading the past: Critical and functional perspectives on time and value*, 247–271, Amsterdam: John Benjamins Publishing Company.

Barwell, R. (2013), Discursive psychology as an alternative perspective on mathematics teacher knowledge, *ZDM – International Journal on Mathematics Education*, 45 (4): 595–606. https://doi.org/10.1007/s11858-013-0508-4.

Barwell, R. (2018), From language as a resource to sources of meaning in multilingual mathematics classrooms, *Journal of Mathematical Behavior*. https://doi.org/10.1016/j.jmathb.2018.02.007.

Bayley, R., H. Hansen-Thomas and J. Langman (2005), 'Language brokering in a middle school science class', in *Proceedings of the 4th International Symposium on Bilingualism*, 223–232, Somerville, MA: Cascadilla Press. http://www.lingref.com/isb/4/016ISB4.PDF.

Bebell, D. and S. E. Stemler (2004), *Reassessing the objectives of educational accountability in Massachusetts: The mismatch between Massachusetts and the MCAS*, San Diego, CA: Paper presented at the annual meeting of the American Educational Research Association.

Benwell, B. and E. H. Stokoe (2006), *Discourse and identity*, Edinburgh: Edinburgh University Press.

Bernstein, B. (1996), *Pedagogy, Symbolic Control and Ideology: Theory, Research, Critique*, Bristol: Taylor & Francis.

Biber, D. (2006), *University language: A corpus-based study of spoken and written registers*, Amsterdam: John Benjamins Publishing Company.

Biber, D., S. Conrad and V. Cortes (2004), If you look at …: Lexical bundles in university teaching and textbooks, *Applied Linguistics*, 25 (3): 371–405.

Biber, D., S. Johansson, G. Leech, S. Conrad and E. Finegan (2006), *Longman grammar of spoken and written English*, London: Longman.

Bilmes, J. (1988), The concept of preference in conversation analysis, *Language in Society*, 17 (2): 161–181.

Blackledge, A. and A. Creese (2014), *Heteroglossia as practice and pedagogy*, Dordrecht: Springer.

Blommaert, J. (2016), 'From mobility to complexity in sociolinguistic theory and method', in N. Coupland (ed.), *Sociolinguistics: Theoretical debates*, Cambridge: Cambridge University Press.

Blommaert, J. and B. Rampton (2011), *Language and superdiversity*, Gottingen. Available at: www.mmg.mpg.de/workingpapers.

Blumer, H. (1969), *Symbolic interactionism: Perspective and method*, Englewood Cliffs, NJ: Prentice-Hall.

Bogdan, R. and S. Biklen (1998), *Qualitative research for education: An introduction to theory and methods*, Boston, MA: Allyn and Bacon.

British Educational Research Association (BERA) (2018), *Ethical guidelines for educational research* (4th edition). Available at: https://www.bera.ac.uk/wp-content/uploads/2018/06/BERA-Ethical-Guidelines-for-Educational-Research_4thEdn_2018.pdf.

Brooks, C. F. (2016), Role, power, ritual, and resistance: A critical discourse analysis of college classroom talk, *Western Journal of Communication*, 80 (3): 348–369. https://doi.org/10.1080/10570314.2015.1098723.

Brooks, R., K. Te Riele and M. Maguire (2014), *Ethics and education research*, London: Sage.

Brown, A. L., D. Ash, M. Rutherford, K. Nakagawa, A. Gordon and J. C. Campione (1993), 'Distributed expertise in the classroom', in G. Salomon (ed.), *Distributed cognitions: Psychological and educational considerations*, 188–228, Cambridge: Cambridge University Press.

Brown, P. and S. C. Levinson (1987), *Politeness: Some universals in language usage*, Cambridge: Cambridge University Press.

Butler, J. (1990), *Gender Trouble*, New York and London: Routledge.

Buzzelli, C. and B. Johnston (2001), Authority, power, and morality in classroom discourse, *Teaching and Teacher Education*, 17 (8), 873–884. DOI: 10.1016/S0742-051X(01)00037-3.

Cameron, D. (2007), Unanswered questions and unquestioned assumptions in the study of language and gender: Female verbal superiority, *Gender and Language*, 1 (1): 15–25.

Cameron, D., E. Frazer, P. Harvey, M. B. H. Rampton and K. Richardson (2018), *Researching language: Issues of power and method*, Abingdon: Routledge.

Canagarajah, S. (2013), *Translingual practice: Global Englishes and cosmopolitan relations*, Abingdon: Routledge.

Carretero, M., M. Asensio and M. Rodríguez-Moneo (2012), *History education and the construction of national identities*, Charlotte, NC: Information Age Publishing.

Carter, S. P. (2007), 'Reading all that white crazy stuff': Black young women unpacking whiteness in a high school British literature classroom, *The Journal of Classroom Interaction*, 42 (1): 42–54.

Cazden, C. B. (1988), *Classroom discourse: The language of teaching and learning*, Portsmouth, NH: Heinemann.

Chambers, A. and I. O'Sullivan (2004), Corpus consultation and advanced learners' writing skills in French, *ReCALL*, 16 (1): 158–172.

Chapman, A. J. (2009), 'Towards an interpretations heuristic: A case study exploration of 16–19 year old students' ideas about explaining variations in historical accounts', EdD dissertation, University of London.

Cheng, W. (2011), *Exploring corpus linguistics*, Abingdon: Routledge.

Chevallard, Y. (1991), *La transposition didactique*, Grenoble: La Pensée Sauvage.

Chin, C. (2006), Classroom interaction in science: Teacher questioning and feedback to students' responses, *International Journal of Science Education*, 28 (11): 1315–1346. https://doi.org/10.1080/09500690600621100.

Cobb, P., M. Gresalfi, and L. L. Hodge (2009), An interpretive scheme for analyzing the identities that students develop in mathematics classrooms, *Journal for Research in Mathematics Education*, 40 (1): 40–68.

Cochran-Smith, M. and S. L. Lytle (2009), *Inquiry as stance: Practitioner research for the next generation*, New York: Teachers College Press.

Creese, A. and A. Blackledge (2011), Separate and flexible bilingualism in complementary schools: Multiple language practices in interrelationship, *Journal of Pragmatics*, 43 (5): 1196–1208. https://doi.org/10.1016/j.pragma.2010.10.006.

Cummins, J. (2000), *Language, power, and pedagogy: Bilingual children in the crossfire* (Vol. 23), Clevedon, UK: Multilingual Matters.

Cummins, J. (2016), A proposal for action: Strategies for recognizing heritage language competence as a learning resource within the mainstream classroom, *The Modern Language Journal*, 89 (4): 585–592.

Cummins, J. and M. Swain (1986), *Bilingualism in education: Aspects of theory, research and practice*, Abingdon: Routledge.

Cuoco, A., E. Paul Goldenberg and J. Mark (1996), Habits of mind: An organizing principle for mathematics curricula, *The Journal of Mathematical Behavior*, 15 (4): 375–402. https://doi.org/10.1016/S0732-3123(96)90023-1.

Davidson, C. (2009), Transcription: Imperatives for qualitative research, *International Journal of Qualitative Methods*, 8 (2): 36–52.

Davies, B. and R. Harré (1990), Positioning: The discursive production of selves, *Journal for the Theory of Social Behaviour*, 20 (1): 43–63.

Davies, B. and R. Harré (1999), 'Positioning and personhood', in B. Davies and R. Harré, *Positioning theory*, 32–52, Oxford: Blackwell Publishers Ltd.

De Fina, A. (2006), 'Discourse and identity', in A. De Fina, D. Schiffrin and M. Bamberg (eds), *Discourse and identity*, 263–282, Cambridge: Cambridge University Press.

De La Paz, S. and D. R. Wissinger (2015), Effects of genre and content knowledge on historical thinking with academically diverse high school students, *The Journal of Experimental Education*, 83 (1): 110–129.

Deckert, S. K. and C. H. Vickers (2011), *An introduction to sociolinguistics: Society and identity*, London: Continuum.

Deem, R. (1978), *Women and schooling*, London: Routledge.

Department for Education (2014), *The National Curriculum in England: Key Stages 3 and 4 framework document*. Available at: https://www.gov.uk/government/publications/national-curriculum-in-england-secondary-curriculum.

Dorling, D. (2010), *Injustice*, Bristol: Policy Press.

Duff, P. A. (2007), Second language socialization as sociocultural theory: Insights and issues, *Language Teaching*, 40 (4): 309–319. https://doi.org/10.1017/S0261444807004508.

Edwards, A. D. and D. P. G. Westgate (1994), *Investigating classroom talk* (2nd edn), London: The Falmer Press.

Edwards, D. and J. Potter (1992), *Discursive psychology*, London: Sage.

Edwards, D. and N. Mercer (1987), *Common knowledge: The development of understanding in the classroom*, Abingdon: Routledge.

Edwards, J. A. and M. D. Lampert (1993), *Talking data: Transcription and coding in discourse research*, Hillsdale, NJ and London: Erlbaum.

Elliott, V. (2017), Gender and the contemporary educational canon in the UK, *International Journal of English Studies*, 17 (2): 45–62.

Elliott, V. (2018), Thinking about the coding process in qualitative data analysis, *The Qualitative Report*, 23 (11): 2850–2861.

Elliott, V. and B. Hore (2016), 'Right nutrition, right values': The construction of food, youth and morality in the UK government 2010–2014, *Cambridge Journal of Education*, 46 (2): 177–193.

Ellis, N. C. and D. Larsen–Freeman, eds (2009), *Language as a complex adaptive system*, Chichester and Malden, MA: Wiley-Blackwell.

Emery, C. (2016), A critical discourse analysis of the New Labour discourse of Social and Emotional Learning (SEL) across schools in England and Wales: Conversations with policymakers, *Education Policy Analysis Archives*, 24 (104), http://dx.doi.org/10.14507/epaa.24.2236.

Enright, E. and M. O'Sullivan (2012), 'Producing different knowledge and producing knowledge differently': Rethinking physical education research and practice through participatory visual methods, *Sport, Education and Society*, 17 (1): 35–55.

Enyedy, N., L. Rubel, V. Castellón, S. Mukhopadhyay, I. Esmonde and W. Secada (2008), Revoicing in a multilingual classroom, *Mathematical Thinking and Learning*, 10 (2): 134–162. https://doi.org/10.1080/10986060701854458.

Erduran, S. (2018), Toulmin's argument pattern as a 'horizon of possibilities' in the study of argumentation in science education, *Cultural Studies of Science Education*, 1–9. Available at: https://doi.org/10.1007/s11422-017-9847-8.

Erduran, S., S. Simon and J. Osborne (2004), TAPping into argumentation: Developments in the application of Toulmin's Argument Pattern for studying science discourse, *Science Education*, 88 (6): 915–933. https://doi.org/10.1002/sce.20012.

Erickson, F. (2004), *Talk and social theory: Ecologies of speaking and listening in everyday life*, Cambridge, UK: Polity Press.

Esmonde, I. (2009), Ideas and identities: Supporting equity in cooperative mathematics learning, *Review of Educational Research* 79 (2): 1008–1043. https://doi.org/10.3102/0034654309332562.

Fairclough, N. (1989), *Language and power*, London and New York: Longman.

Fairclough, N. and R. Wodak (1997), 'Critical discourse analysis: An overview', in T. A. van Dijk (ed.), *Discourse and interaction*, 258–284, London: Sage.

Farr, F. (2016), *The Routledge handbook of language learning and technology*, Abingdon: Routledge.

Fitzgerald, T. (2012), 'Documents and documentary analysis', in A. R. Briggs, M. Morrison and M. Coleman (eds), *Research methods in educational leadership and management*, 296–308, London: Sage.

Fitzgerald, T., M. Hackling and V. Dawson (2013), Through the viewfinder: Reflecting on the collection and analysis of classroom video data, *International Journal of Qualitative Methods*, 52–64. DOI: 10.1177/160940691301200127.

Flanders, N. A. (1960), *Analyzing teacher behavior*, Reading, MA: Addison-Wesley.

Flewitt, R. (2006), Using video to investigate preschool classroom interaction: Education research assumptions and methodological practices, *Visual Communication*, 5 (1): 25–50.

Flores, N. (2016), A tale of two visions: Hegemonic whiteness and bilingual education, *Educational Policy*, 30 (1): 13–38. https://doi.org/10.1177/0895904815616482.

Forman, E. A., J. Larreamendy-Joerns, M. K. Stein and C. A. Brown (1998), 'You're going to want to find out which and prove it': Collective argumentation in a mathematics classroom, *Learning and Instruction*, 8 (6): 527–548. https://doi.org/10.1016/S0959-4752(98)00033-4.

Forrester, M. A. and C. D. Pike (1998), Learning to estimate in the mathematics classroom: A conversation-analytic approach, *Journal for Research in Mathematics Education*, 29 (3): 334–356.

Fortanet, I. (2004), The use of 'we' in university lectures: Reference and function, *English for Specific Purposes*, 23 (1): 45–66. https://doi.org/10.1016/S0889-4906(03)00018-8.

Fortanet, I. (2006), 'Interaction in academic spoken English: The use if "I" and "you" in the MICASE', in E. Arno Macia, A. Soler Cervera and C. Rueda Ramos (eds), *Information technology in languages for specific purposes: Issues and propsects*, 35–52, New York: Springer.

Foucault, M. (1977), *Discipline and punish: The birth of the prison*, New York: Pantheon.

Foucault, M. (1990), *The history of sexuality: Volume 1, an introduction*, trans. R. Hurley, New York: Vintage Books.

Foucault, M. (1994), 'An interview with Michel Foucault', in J. D. Faubion (ed.), *Power*, Vol. 3, 239–297, New York: The New Press.

García, O. and L. Wei (2014), *Translanguaging: Language, bilingualism and education*, Basingstoke: Palgrave.

García, O. and N. Kano (2014), 'Translanguaging as process and pedagogy: Developing the English writing of Japanese students in the US', in J. Conteh and G. Meier (eds), *The multilingual turn in languages education: Opportunities and challenges*, 258–277, Bristol: Multilingual Matters.

Garfinkel, H. (1967), *Studies in ethnomethodology*, Englewood Cliffs, NJ: Prentice-Hall.

Gee, J. P. (1999), *An introduction to discourse analysis: Theory and methods*, London: Routledge.

Gee, J. P. (2000), Chapter 3: Identity as an analytic lens for research in education, *Review of Research in Education*, 25 (1): 99–125. https://doi.org/10.3102/0091732X025001099.

Gilquin, G., S. Granger and M. Paquot (2007), Learner corpora: The missing link in EAP pedagogy, *Journal of English for Academic Purposes*, 6 (4): 319–335. https://doi.org/10.1016/j.jeap.2007.09.007

Giovanelli, M. (2016), 'Text World Theory as cognitive grammatics: A pedagogical application in the secondary classroom', in J. Gavins and E. Lahey (eds), *World-building: Discourse in the mind*, 109–126, London: Bloomsbury.

Giovanelli, M. (2017), Readers building fictional worlds: Visual representations, *Poetry, and Cognition, Literacy*, 51 (1): 26–35.

Glaser, B. G. and A. L. Strauss (1967), *The discovery of grounded theory*, New York: Aldine.

Goffman, E. (1955), On face-work: An analysis of ritual elements in social interaction, *Psychiatry*, 18 (3): 213–231.

Goffman, E. (1981), *Forms of talk*, Oxford: Blackwell.

Goodwin, C. (2000), Action and embodiment within situated human interaction, *Journal of Pragmatics*, 32: 1489–1522.

Graff, J. M. (2010), Countering narratives: Teachers' discourses about immigrants and their experiences within the realm of children's and young adult literature, *English Teaching: Practice and Critique*, 9 (3): 106–131.

Gray, J. (2002), *Men are from Mars, women are from Venus*, London: Harper Collins.

Green, J., M. Franquiz and C. Dixon (1997), The myth of the objective transcript: Transcribing as a situated act, *Tesol Quarterly*, 31 (1): 172–176.

Greenhalgh, J. (2014), 'Till we hear the last all clear': Gender and the presentation of self in young girls' writing about the bombing of Hull during the Second World War, *Gender and History*, 26 (1): 167–183.

Gries, S. T. (2016), *Quantitative corpus linguistics with R: A practical introduction* (2nd edn), London: Routledge.

Groundwater-Smith, S. and N. Mockler (2007), Ethics in practitioner research: An issue of quality, *Research Papers in Education*, 22 (2): 199–211.

Gumperz, J. J. (1964), Linguistic and social interaction in two communities, *American Anthropologist*, 66 (6): 137–153. https://doi.org/10.2307/668168.

Gunter, H., C. Mills and D. Hall, eds (2014), *Education policy research: Design and practice at a time of rapid reform*, London: Bloomsbury.

Halliday, M. A. K. (1961), Categories of the theory of grammar, *Word*, 17 (2): 241–292.

Halliday, M. A. K. (1993), Towards a language-based learning theory of learning, *Linguistics and Education*, 5: 93–116.

Hardaker, C. (2015), 'I refuse to respond to this obvious troll': An overview of responses to (perceived) trolling, *Corpora*, 10 (2): 201–229.

Harper, D. (2002), Talking about pictures: A case for photo elicitation, *Visual Studies*, 17 (1): 13–26.

Harré, R. (2012), 'Positioning theory: Moral dimensions of socialcultural spychology', in J. Valsiner (ed.), *The Oxford handbook of culture and psychology*, 191–206, New York: Oxford University Press.

Harré, R. and L. van Langenhove (1999), *Positioning theory: Moral contexts of intentional action*, Oxford: Blackwell.

Harré, R., F. M. Moghaddam, T. P. Cairnie, D. Rothbart and S. R. Sabat (2009), Recent advances in positioning theory, *Theory and Psychology*, 19 (1): 5–31. https://doi.org/10.1177/0959354308101417.

Haw, K. and M. Hadfield (2011), *Video in social science research: Functions and forms*, Abingdon: Routledge.

Heath, C., J. Hindmarsh and P. Luff (2010), *Video in qualitative research*, London: Sage.

Heller, V. (2014), Discursive practices in family dinner talk and classroom discourse: A contextual comparison, *Learning, Culture and Social Interaction*, 3 (2): 134–145.

Heller, V. (2017), Managing knowledge claims in classroom discourse: The public construction of a homogeneous epistemic status, *Classroom Discourse*, 8 (2): 156–174. https://doi.org/10.1080/19463014.2017.1 328699.

Herbel-Eisenmann, B. A. A., D. Wagner, K. R. R. Johnson, H. Suh and H. Figueras (2015), Positioning in mathematics education: Revelations on an imported theory, *Educational Studies in Mathematics*, 89 (2): 185–204. https://doi.org/10.1007/s10649-014-9588-5.

Herbel-Eisenmann, B. and D. Wagner (2010), Appraising lexical bundles in mathematics classroom discourse: Obligation and choice, *Educational Studies in Mathematics*, 75 (1): 43–63. https://doi.org/10.1007/s10649-010-9240-y.

Herbel-Eisenmann, B., D. Wagner and V. Cortes (2010), Lexical bundle analysis in mathematics classroom discourse: The significance of stance, *Educational Studies in Mathematics*, 75 (1): 23–42. https://doi.org/10.1007/s10649-010-9253-6.

Heritage, J. (1984), *Garfinkel and Ethnomethodology*, New York: Polity Press.

Heritage, J. (1986), *Exposed working on understanding in conversation and news interviews*: Unpublished.

Heritage, J. (2012a), Epistemics in action: Action formation and territories of knowledge, *Research on Language and Social Interaction*, 45 (1): 1–29. https://doi.org/10.1080/08351813.2012.646684.

Heritage, J. (2012b), The epistemic engine: Sequence organization and territories of knowledge, *Research on Language and Social Interaction*, 45 (1): 30–52. https://doi.org/10.1080/08351813.2012.646685.

Heritage, J. (2013), Action formation and its epistemic (and other) backgrounds, *Discourse Studies*, 15 (5): 551–578. https://doi.org/10.1177/1461445613501449.

Hirsch Jr, E. D., (1987), *Cultural literacy: What every American needs to know*, Boston, MA: Houghton Mifflin.

Holland, D., W. Lachicotte, D. Skinner and C. Cain (1998), *Identity and agency in cultural worlds*, Cambridge, MA: Harvard University Press.

Hollway, W. (1983), 'Heterosexual sex: Power and desire for the other', in S. Cartledge and J. Ryan (eds), *Sex and love: New thoughts on old contradictions*, 124–140, London: Women's Press.

Holmes, J. (2006), Sharing a laugh: Pragmatic aspects of humor and gender in the workplace, *Journal of Pragmatics*, 38 (1), 26–50.

Hore, B. (2014), *How do counselling psychologists in the UK construct their responsibilities to the widerworld? A Foucauldian discourse analysis*. Unpublished thesis, London Metropolitan University.

Hunston, S. (2002). *Corpora in applied linguistics*, Cambridge: Cambridge University Press.

Hutchby, I. and R. Wooffitt (1998), *Conversation analysis: Principles, practices and applications*, Cambridge: Polity.

Hutchins, E. (1995), *Cognition in the wild*, Cambridge, MA: MIT Press.

Hyland, K. (2006), *English for academic purposes*, London: Routledge.

Hyland, K. and L. Hamp-Lyons (2002), EAP: Issues and directions, *Journal of English for Academic Purposes*, 1 (1): 1–12. https://doi.org/10.1016/S1475-1585(02)00002-4.

Ingram, J. (2018), Moving forward with ethnomethodological approaches to analysing mathematics classroom interactions, *ZDM – Mathematics Education*. https://doi.org/10.1007/s11858-018-0951-3.

Ingram, J. and V. Elliott (2014), Turn taking and 'wait time' in classroom interactions, *Journal of Pragmatics*, 62: 1–12. https://doi.org/10.1016/j.pragma.2013.12.002.

Ingram, J. and V. Elliott (2016), A critical analysis of the role of wait time in classroom interactions and the effects on student and teacher interactional behaviours, *Cambridge Journal of Education*, 46 (1): 1–17. https://doi.org/10.1080/0305764X.2015.1009365.

Ingram, J., A. Pitt and F. Baldry (2015), Handling errors as they arise in whole-class interactions, *Research in Mathematics Education*, 17 (3): 183–197. https://doi.org/10.1080/14794802.2015.1098562.

Ingram, J., N. Andrews and A. Pitt (2018), 'Making student explanations relevant in whole class discussion', in J. N. N. Moschkovich, D. Wagner, A. Bose, J. Rodrigues Mendes and M. Schuette (eds), *Language and communication in mathematics educaton: International perspectives*, 51–64, Champaign: Springer.

Ingram, J., N. Andrews and A. Pitt (2019), When students offer explanations without the teacher explicilty asking them to, *Educational Studies in Mathematics*. DOI: 10.1007/s10649-018-9873-9.

Ingram, J., P. Sammons and A. Lindorff (2018), *Observing effective mathematics teaching: A review of the literature*. Education Development Trust, available at: https://www.educationdevelopmenttrust.com/~/media/EDT/Reports/Research/2018/r-observing-mathematics-2018.pdf (accessed 13 December 2018).

Jefferson, G. (2004), Glossary of transcript symbols with an introduction, *Pragmatics and beyond New Series*, 125: 13–34.

Jeffries, L. (2008), *Critical stylistics*, Basingstoke: Palgrave Macmillan.

Jennings, P. A., J. L. Brown, J. L. Frank, S. Doyle, Y. Oh, R. Davis, R. D. Rasheed, A. DeWeese, A. A. DeMauro, H. Cham and M. T. Greenberg

(2017), Impacts of the CARE for teachers program on teachers' social and emotional competence and classroom interactions, *Journal of Educational Psychology*, 109 (7): 1010–1030.

Jewitt, C. (2009), *The Routledge handbook of multimodal analysis*, London: Routledge.

Jobeen, A., B. Kazemian and M. Shahbaz (2015), The role of error analysis in teaching and learning of second and foreign language, *Education and Linguistics Research*, 1 (2): 52–62. DOI: 10.5296/elr.v1i1.8189.

Jordan, B. and A. Henderson (2009), Interaction analysis: Foundations and practice, *The Journal of the Learning Sciences*, 4 (1): 39–103. https://doi.org/10.1207/s15327809jls0401.

Jørgensen, J. N., M. S. Karrebæk, L. M. Madsen and J. S. Møller (2011), Polylanguaging in superdiveristy, *Diversities*, 13 (2): 23–38.

Kääntä, L. (2014), From noticing to initiating correction: Students' epistemic displays in instructional interaction, *Journal of Pragmatics*, 66: 86–105. https://doi.org/10.1016/j.pragma.2014.02.010.

Karlsson, A. (2015), Code-switching as a linguistic resource in the multilingual science classroom, *Electronic Proceedings of the ESERA 2015 Conference, Science Education Research: Engaging Learners for a Sustainable Future*: 1820–1831.

Katz, J. (2016), *Speaking American: How y'all, youse, and you guys talk: A visual guide*, New York: Houghton Mifflin Harcourt.

Kemmis, S. (2006), Participatory action research and the public sphere, *Educational Action Research*, 14 (4): 459–476.

Kemmis, S. and R. McTaggart (2005), 'Participatory action research: Communicative action and the public sphere', in N. K. Denzin and Y. S. Lincoln (eds), *The Sage handbook of qualitative research*, 559–603, Thousand Oaks, CA: Sage Publications Ltd.

Kerssen-Griep, J., A. R. Tress and J. A. Hess (2008), Attentive facework during instructional feedback: Key to perceiving mentorship and an optimal learning environment, *Communication Education*, 57 (3): 312–332. DOI: 10.1080/03634520802027347

Kim, J. I. and K. M. Viesca (2016), Three reading-intervention teachers' identity positioning and practices to motivate and engage emergent bilinguals in an urban middle school, *Teaching and Teacher Education*, 55: 122–132. https://doi.org/10.1016/j.tate.2016.01.003.

Kim, M. and W. M. Roth (2018), Dialogical argumentation in elementary science classrooms, *Cultural Studies of Science Education*. https://doi.org/10.1007/s11422-017-9846-9.

Kim, M. and W. Roth (2014), Argumentation as / in / for dialogical relation: A case study from elementary school science, *Pedagogies: An International Journal*, 9: 300–321. https://doi.org/10.1080/155448 0X.2014.955498.

Koole, T. (2012), The epistemics of student problems: Explaining mathematics in a multi-lingual class, *Journal of Pragmatics*, 44 (13): 1902–1916. https://doi.org/10.1016/j.pragma.2012.08.006.

Kress, G. (2009), 'What is mode?' in C. Jewitt (ed.), *The Routledge handbook of multimodal analysis*, 54–67, London: Routledge.

Kress, G., C. Jewitt, J. Ogborn and C. Tsatsarelis (2001), *Multimodal teaching and learning: The rhetorics of the science classroom*, London: Continuum.

Krummheuer, G. (2000), Mathematics learning in narrative classroom cultures: Studies of argumentation in primary mathematics education, *For the Learning of Mathematics*, 20 (1): 22–32.

Krummheuer, G. (2007), Argumentation and participation in the primary mathematics classroom. Two episodes and related theoretical abductions, *Journal of Mathematical Behavior*, 26 (1): 60–82. https://doi.org/10.1016/j.jmathb.2007.02.001.

Kvale, S. (2008), *Doing Interviews*, London: Sage.

Lambert, R. (2015), Constructing and resisting disability in mathematics classrooms: A case study exploring the impact of different pedagogies, *Educational Studies in Mathematics*, 89 (1): 1–18. https://doi.org/10.1007/s10649-014-9587-6.

Lee, Y-A. (2008), Yes-No questions in the third-turn position: Pedagogical discourse processes, *Discourse Processes*, 45 (3): 237–262. http://dx.doi.org/10.1080/01638530701739215.

Lemke, J. L. (1990), *Talking science: Language, learning, and values*, Norwood, NJ: Ablex.

Lemke, J. L. (2000), Across the scales of time: Artifacts, activities and meanings in ecosocial systems, *Mind, Culture and Activity*, 7 (4): 273–290.

Liebscher, G. and J. Dailey-O'Cain (2003), Conversational repair as a role-defining mechanism in classroom interaction, *The Modern Language Journal*, 87 (3): 375–390. https://doi.org/10.1111/1540-4781.00196.

Lillis, T. (2013), *Sociolinguistics of writing*, Edinburgh: Edinburgh University Press.

Liu, D. (2005), Plagiarism in ESOL students: Is cultural conditioning truly the major culprit? *ELT Journal*, 59 (3): 234–241.

Macbeth, D. (2011), Understanding understanding as an instructional matter, *Journal of Pragmatics*, 43 (2): 438–451. https://doi.org/10.1016/j.pragma.2008.12.006.

Mäkitalo, A. and R. Säljö (2002), Talk in institutional context and institutional context in talk: Categories as situated practices, *Text*, 22 (1): 57–82.

Makoni, S. and A. Pennycook (2012), 'Disinventing multilingualism: From monological multilingualism to multilingua francas', in M. Martin-

Jones, A. Blackledge and A. Creese (eds), *The Routledge handbook of multilingualism*, London: Routledge.

Marin, R. (1992), Grunge: A success story, *The New York Times*, November 15: 9.

Martin-Beltrán, M. (2010), The two-way language bridge: Co-constructing bilingual language learning opportunities, *The Modern Language Journal*, 94 (ii): 254–277.

Martinez, D. C., P. Z. Morales and U. S. Aldana (2017), Leveraging students' communicative repertoires as a tool for equitable learning, *Review of Research in Education*, 41 (1): 477–499. https://doi.org/10.3102/0091732X17691741.

Martínez, R. A., L. Durán and M. Hikida (2017), Becoming 'Spanish Learners': Identity and interaction among multilingual children in a Spanish-English dual language classroom, *International Multilingual Research Journal*, 11 (3): 167–183. https://doi.org/10.1080/19313152.2017.1330065.

Martínez-Roldán, C. M. and G. Malavé (2004), Language ideologies mediating literacy and identity in bilingual contexts, *Journal of Early Childhood Literacy*, 4 (2): 155–180. https://doi.org/10.1177/1468798404044514.

Mason, J. and M. Giovanelli (2017), 'What do you think?' Let me tell you: Discourse about texts and the literature classroom, *Changing English*, 24 (3): 318–329.

Mayo, E. (1949), *Hawthorne and the western electric company, the social problems of an industrial civilisation*, Philadelphia: Routledge.

McAvoy, J. (2016), 'Discursive psychology and the production of identity in language practices', in S. Preece (ed.), *The Routledge handbook of language and identity*, 98–112, London: Routledge.

McDowell, J. and R. Klattenberg (2018), Does gender matter? A cross-national investigation of primary class-room discipline, *Gender and Education*. DOI: 10.1080/09540253.2018.1458078.

McHoul, A. (1978), The organization of turns at formal talk in the classroom, *Language in Society*, 7 (2): 183–213.

McHoul, A. (1990), The organization of repair in classroom talk, *Language in Society*, 19 (3): 349–377.

Mehan, H. (1979), *Learning lessons: Social organization in the classroom*, Cambridge, MA: Harvard University Press.

Mercer, N. (2000), *Words and minds: How we use language to think together*, London: Routledge.

Mercer, N. (2002), 'Researching common knowledge: Studying the content and context of educational discourse', in G. Walford (ed.), *Doing educational research*, 53–70, Abingdon: Routledge.

Michaels, S. and C. O'Connor (2015), 'Conceptualizing talk moves as tools: Professional development approaches for academically productive discussion', in L. B. Resnick, C. Asterhan and S. N. Clarke (eds), *Socializing intelligence through talk and dialogue*, 347–362, Washington: American Educational Research Association.

Miles, M. B. and A. M. Huberman (1994), *Qualitative data analysis: An expanded sourcebook*, London: Sage.

Miles, M. B., A. M. Huberman and J. Saldana (2013), *Qualitative data analysis*, London: Sage.

Mockler, N. (2014), When 'research ethics' become 'everyday ethics': The intersection of inquiry and practice in practitioner research, *Educational Action Research*, 22 (2): 146–158.

Moghaddam, F. M., R. Harré and N. Lee (2008), 'Positioning and conflict: An introduction', in F. M. Moghaddam, R. Harré and N. Lee (eds), *Global conflict resolution through positioning analysis*, 3–20, New York: Springer.

Murphy, V. A. (2014), *Second language learning in the early school years: Trends and contexts*, Oxford: Oxford University Press.

Myers-Scotton, C. (2006), *Multiple voices: An introduction to bilingualism*, Malden, MA: Blackwell Pub.

Neuendorf, K. A. (2016). *The content analysis guidebook*, Thousand Oaks, CA: SAGE.

Nichols, T. (2017), *The death of expertise: The campaign against established knowledge and why it matters*, New York: Oxford University Press.

Nind, M., A. Curtin and K. Hall (2016), *Research methods for pedagogy*, London: Bloomsbury.

O'Boyle, A. (2014), 'You' and 'I' in university seminars and spoken learner discourse, *Journal of English for Academic Purposes*, 16: 40–56. https://doi.org/10.1016/j.jeap.2014.08.003.

O'Hallaron, C. L. and M. J. Schleppegrell (2016), 'Voice' in children's science arguments: Aligning assessment criteria with genre and discipline, *Assessing Writing*, 30: 63–73.

O'Keeffe, A. and M. McCarthy, eds (2010), *The Routledge handbook of corpus linguistics*, Abingdon: Routledge.

Oancea, A. E, and J. Furlong (2005) 'Assessing quality in applied and practice-based educational research: A framework for discussion', in *Report to the economic and social research council*, Oxford: Oxford University Department of Educational Studies.

OECD (2018), *Teaching in Focus #20: What does teaching look like: A new video study*. 17 January 2018. Available at: https://www.oecd-ilibrary.org/education/what-does-teaching-look-like_948427dc-en (accessed 13 December 2018). https://doi.org/10.1787/948427dc-en.

Ortega, L. (2005), For what and for whom is our research? The ethical as transformative lens in instructed SLA, *The Modern Language Journal*, 89 (3): 427–443.

Park, M. S. (2012), Code-switching and translanguaging: Potential functions in multilingual classrooms, *TESOL and Applied Linguistics*, 13 (2): 50–52. https://doi.org/10.1080/09500782.2013.788022.

Piaget, J. (1965), *The moral judgement of the child*, New York: Free Press. (Original work published in 1932).

Piaget, J. (1995), *Sociological studies*, London: Routledge. (Original work published 1977).

Pillay, P. and S. Maistry (2018), The 'firstness' of male as automatic ordering: Gendered discourse in Southern African business studies school textbooks, *The Journal for Transdisciplinary Research in Southern Africa*, 14 (2): 1–9.

Planas, N. (2011), Language identities in students' writings about group work in their mathematics classroom, *Language and Education*, 25 (2): 129–146. https://doi.org/10.1080/09500782.2011.552725.

Planas, N. and M. Setati (2009), Bilingual students using their languages in the learning of mathematics: A sociolinguistic approach to bilingualism, *Mathematics Education Research Journal*, 21 (3): 36–59.

Pollitt, R., C. Cohrssen, A. Church and S. Wright (2015), Thirty-one is a lot! Assessing four-year-old children's number knowledge during an open-ended activity, *Australasian Journal of Early Childhood*, 40 (1): 13–22.

Pontier, R. and M. Gort (2016), Coordinated translanguaging pedagogy as distributed cognition: A case study of two dual language bilingual education preschool coteachers' languaging practices during shared book readings, *International Multilingual Research Journal*, 10 (2): 89–106. https://doi.org/10.1080/19313152.2016.1150732.

Potter, J. and M. Wetherell (1987), *Discourse and social psychology*, London: Sage.

Preece, S. (2016), *The Routledge handbook of language and identity*, London: Routledge.

Prior, L. (2013), 'The role of documents in social research', in S. Delamont (ed.), *Handbook of qualitative research in education*, 426–438, Cheltenham: Edward Elgar Publishing.

Psathas, G. (1995), *Conversation analysis*, London: Sage.

Radford, J., P. Blatchford and R. Webster (2011), Opening up and closing down: How teachers and TAs manage turn-taking, topic and repair in mathematics lessons, *Learning and Instruction*, 21 (5): 625–635. https://doi.org/10.1016/j.learninstruc.2011.01.004.

Reyes, I. (2004), Functions of code switching in schoolchildren's conversations, *Bilingual Research Journal*, 28 (1): 77–98. https://doi.org/10.1080/15235882.2004.10162613.

Ricento, T. (2005), Problems with the 'language-as-resource' discourse in the promotion of heritage languages in the U.S.A, *Journal of Sociolinguistics*, 9 (3): 348–368. https://doi.org/10.1111/j.1360-6441.2005.00296.x.

Richards, K. (2006), 'Being the teacher': Identity and classroom
conversation, *Applied Linguistics*, 27 (1): 51–77. https://doi.
org/10.1093/applin/ami041.

Rogers, R., E. Malancharuvil-Berkes, M. Mosley, D. Hui and G. O. G.
Joseph (2005), Critical discourse analysis: A review of the literature,
Review of Educational Research, 75 (3): 365–415. http://dx.doi.
org/10.3102/00346543075003365.

Rowe, M. B. (1972), *Wait-Time and rewards as instructional variables:
Their influence on language, logic and fate control*, paper presented at
the annual meeting of the *National Association for Research in Science
Teaching*, Chicago, Illinois.

Ruitenberg, C. W. and D. C. Phillips, eds (2011), *Education, culture
and epistemological diversity: Mapping a disputed terrain* (Vol. 2),
Dordrecht: Springer.

Ruiz, R. (1984), Orientations in language planning, *NABE Journal*, 8 (2):
15–34.

Rumelhart, D. E. (2017), 'Schemata: The building blocks of cognition',
in R. J. Spiro, B. C. Bruce and W. F. Brewer (eds), *Theoretical issues in
reading comprehension*, 33–58, Abingdon: Routledge.

Rymes, B. (2015), *Classroom discourse analysis: A tool for critical
reflection*, New York: Routledge.

Sacks, H. (1992), *Lectures on conversation*, Oxford: Blackwell.

Sacks, H., E. A. Schegloff and G. Jefferson (1974), A simplest systematics
for the organization of turn-taking for conversation, *Language*, 50 (4):
696–735.

Saldaña, J. (2015), *The coding manual for qualitative researchers*,
London: SAGE.

Saxena, M. and M. Martin-Jones (2013), Multilingual resources
in classroom interaction: Ethnographic and discourse analytic
perspectives, *Language and Education*, 27 (4): 285–297. https://doi.org/
10.1080/09500782.2013.788020.

Schaenen, I. (2010), 'Genre means …': A critical discourse analysis of fourth
grade talk about genre, *Critical Inquiry in Language Studies*, 7 (1):
28–53.

Schall-Leckrone, L. and D. Barron (2018), 'Apprenticing students and
teachers into historical content, language, and thinking through genre
pedagogy', in L. C. de Oliviera and K. M. Obenchain (eds), *Teaching
history and social studies to English language learners*, 205–231,
Champaign: Palgrave Macmillan.

Schegloff, E. A. (1997), Whose text? Whose context? *Discourse and
Society*, 8 (2): 165–187.

Schegloff, E. A. (2007), *Sequence organization in interaction: A primer in
conversation analysis*, Cambridge: Cambridge University Press.

Schegloff, E. A. and H. Sacks (1973), Opening up closings, *Semiotica*, 8 (4): 289–327. https://doi.org/10.1515/semi.1973.8.4.289.

Schuck, S. and M. Kearney (2006), Using digital video as a research tool: Ethical issues for researchers, *Journal of Educational Multimedia and Hypermedia*, 15 (4): 447–463.

Schwarz, B. B., T. Dreyfus and R. Hershkowitz, eds (2009), *Transformation of knowledge through classroom interaction*, Abingdon: Routledge.

Scott, E. C. and G. Branch (2003), Evolution: What's wrong with 'teaching the controversy', *Trends in Ecology and Evolution*, 18 (10): 499–502.

Scott, J. (1990), *A matter of record: Documentary sources in social research*, Cambridge: Polity Press.

Scott, M. (2008), *WordSmith tools*, Liverpool: Lexical Analysis Software.

Scott, M. and C. Tribble (2006), *Textual patterns*, Amsterdam: John Benjamins Publishing Company.

Seedhouse, P. (2005), Conversation analysis and language learning, *Language Teaching*, 38 (4): 165–187. https://doi.org/10.1017/S0261444805003010.

Setati, M. and J. Adler (2000), Between languages and discourses: Language practices in primary multilingual mathematics classrooms in South Africa, *Educational Studies in Mathematics*, 43 (1): 243–269. https://doi.org/10.1023/A:1011996002062.

Sfard, A. and A. Prusak (2005), Telling identities: In search of an analytic tool for investigating learning as a culturally shaped activity, *Educational Researcher*, 34 (4): 14–22. https://doi.org/10.3102/0013189X034004014.

Sharma, A. and C. A. Buxton (2015), Human-nature relationships in school science: A critical discourse analysis of a middle-grade science textbook, *Science Education*, 99 (2): 260–281.

Sharma, B. K. (2013), Enactment of teacher identity in resolving student disagreements in small group peer interactions, *Linguistics and Education*, 24 (2): 247–259. https://doi.org/10.1016/j.linged.2012.09.002.

Shulman, L. S. (1986), Those who understand: Knowledge growth in teaching, *Educational Researcher*, 15 (2): 4–14. https://doi.org/10.3102/0013189X015002004.

Shulman, L. S. (1987), Knowledge and teaching: Foundations of the new reform, *Harvard Educational Review*, 57 (1): 1–23. https://doi.org/10.17763/haer.57.1.j463w79r56455411.

Sidnell, J. (2010), *Conversation analysis: An introduction*, Chichester: Wiley-Blackwell.

Sidnell, J. and T. Stivers (2012), *The handbook of conversation analysis*, Oxford: Wiley-Blackwell.

Sinclair, J. (1991), *Corpus, concordance, collocation*, Oxford: Oxford University Press.

Sinclair, J. M. H. and M. Coulthard (1975), *Towards an analysis of discourse: The English used by teachers and pupils*, London: Oxford University Press.

Slocum, N. and L. van Langenhove (2004), The meaning of regional integration: Introducing positioning theory in regional integration studies, *Journal of European Integration*, 26 (3): 227–252. https://doi.org/10.1080/0703633042000261625.

Solomon, Y. (2007), Not belonging? What makes a functional learner identity in undergraduate mathematics? *Studies in Higher Education*, 32 (1): 37–41. https://doi.org/10.1080/03075070601099473.

Spolsky, B. (1998), *Sociolinguistics*, Oxford: Oxford University Press.

Spotti, M. and J. Blommaert (2016), 'Bilingualism, multilingualism, globalization, and superdiversity: Toward sociolinguistic repertoire', in O. Garcia, N. Flores and M. Spotti (eds), *The Oxford handbook of language and society*, 161–178, Oxford: Oxford University Press.

Stake, R. (1995), *The art of case study research*, Thousand Oaks, CA: Sage.

Stivers, T., L. Mondada and J. Steensig (2011), Knowledge, morality and affiliation in social interaction, *The morality of knowledge in conversation*, 3–24. https://doi.org/10.1017/CBO9780511921674.002.

Stokoe, E. (2012), Moving forward with membership categorization analysis: Methods for systematic analysis, *Discourse Studies*, 14(3): 277–303. https://doi.org/10.1177/1461445612441534.

Stoskopf, A. and A. Bermudez (2017), The sounds of silence: American history textbook representations of non-violence and the Abolition Movement, *Journal of Peace Education*, 14 (1): 92–113.

Stylianou, P. and M. Zembylas (2018), Dealing with the concepts of 'grief' and 'grieving' in the classroom: Children's perceptions, emotions, and behaviour, *OMEGA-Journal of Death and Dying*, 77 (3): 240–266.

Sundaram, V. and H. Sauntson (2016), Discursive silences: Using critical linguistic and qualitative analysis to explore the continued absence of pleasure in sex and relationships education in England, *Sex Education*, 16 (3), 240–254.

Svendsen, A. M. and J. T. Svendsen (2016), Teacher or coach? How logics from the field of sports contribute to the construction of knowledge in physical education teacher education pedagogical discourse through educational texts, *Sport, Education and Society*, 21 (5): 796–810.

Tang, K. S. (2017), Analyzing teachers' use of Metadiscourse: The missing element in classroom discourse analysis, *Science Education*, 101 (4): 548–583. https://doi.org/10.1002/sce.21275.

Te Molder, H. and J. Potter (2005), *Conversation and cognition*, Cambridge: Cambridge University Press.

Ten Have, P. (2007), *Doing conversation analysis* (2nd edn), London: Sage.

Thomas, E. E. (2015), 'We always talk about race': Navigating race talk dilemmas in the teaching of literature, *Research in the Teaching of English*, 50 (2): 154–175.

Thornbury, S. (2010), 'What can a corpus tell us about discourse', in A. O'Keeffe and M. McMarthy (eds), *The Routledge handbook of corpus linguistics*, 270–287, Abingdon: Routledge.

Tiberghien, A. and L. Malkoun (2009), 'The construction of physics knowledge in the classroom from different perspectives', in B. B. Schwarz, T. Dreyfus and R. Hershkowitz (eds), *Transformation of knowledge through classroom interaction*, 42–56, London; New York: Routledge.

Turnbull, W. (2003), *Language in action: Psychological models of conversation*, New York, NY: Psychology Press.

van Dijk, T. A. (2012), 'Discourse and knowledge', in J. P. Gee and M. Handford (eds), *The Routledge handbook of discourse analysis*, 587–603, London; New York: Routledge.

van Langenhove, L. and R. Harré (1999), 'Introducing positioning theory', in R. Harré and L. van Langenhove (eds), *Positioning theory*, 14–31. https://doi.org/10.1002/asi.20002.

van Lier, L. (2006), *The ecology and semiotics of language learning: A sociocultural perspective*, Champaign: Springer.

Vande Kopple, W. J. (2012), The importance of studying metadiscourse, *Applied Research in English*, 1 (2): 37–44. https://doi.org/10.1111/j.1530-2415.2011.01276.x.

Vertovec, S. (2007), Super-diversity and its implications, *Ethnic and Racial Studies*, 30 (6): 1024–1054. https://doi.org/10.1080/01419870701599465.

Vetter, A. (2010), Positioning students as readers and writers through talk in a high school English classroom, *English Education*, 43 (1): 33–64.

Wächter, L. B. and F. Maiworm (2008), English-taught programmes in European higher education: The state of play in 2014, *ACA Papers on International Cooperation in Education*. Available at: https://www.lemmens.de/dateien/medien/buecher-ebooks/aca/2014_english_taught.pdf.

Walford, G. (2001) *Doing qualitative educational research: A personal guide to the research process*, London: Continuum.

Walton, D. N. (1988), Burden of proof, *Argumentation*, 2 (2): 233–254. https://doi.org/10.2139/ssrn.1954006.

Wells, G. (1993), Reevaluating the IRF sequence: A proposal for the articulation of theories of activity and discourse for the analysis of teaching and learning in the classroom, *Linguistics in Education*, 5: 1–37.

Wenger, E. (1999), *Communities of practice: Learning, meaning, and identity*, Cambridge: Cambridge University Press.

Whitty, G. (1985), *Sociology and school knowledge: Curriculum theory, research and politics*, London: Methuen.

Widdowson, H. G. (2000), On the limitations of linguistics applied, *Applied Linguistics*, 21 (1): 3–25. https://doi.org/10.1093/applin/21.1.3.

Wiley, J. and J. Voss (1999), Constructing arguments from multiple sources: Tasks that promote understanding and not just memory for text, *Journal of Educational Psychology*, 91: 301–311.

Wodak, R. (2013) *Critical discourse analysis*. London: SAGE.

Wodak, R. (2014), 'Critical discourse analysis', in C. Leung and B. Street (eds), *The Routledge companion to English studies*, 302–316, London: Routledge.

Wodak, R. and M. Meyer (eds) (2009), *Methods for critical discourse analysis* (2nd edn), London: Sage.

Wood, C., S. Meachem, S. Bowyer, E. Jackson, M. L. Tarczynski-Bowles and B. Plester (2011), A longitudinal study of children's text messaging and literacy development, *British Journal of Psychology*, 102 (3): 431–442.

Wood, J. M. (2007), Understanding and computing Cohen's kappa: A tutorial, *WebPsychEmpiricist*. Web Journal at http://wpe.info/.

Wood, M. B. (2013), Mathematical micro-identities: Moment-to-moment positioning and learning in a fourth-grade classroom, *Journal for Research in Mathematics Education*, 44 (5): 775–808. https://doi.org/10.5951/jresematheduc.44.5.0775.

Yoon, B. (2008), Uninvited guests: The influence of teachers' roles and pedagogies on the positioning of English language learners in the regular classroom, *American Educational Research Journal*, 45 (2): 495–522. https://doi.org/10.3102/0002831208316200.

Young, M. and J. Muller (2013), On the powers of powerful knowledge, *Review of Education*, 1 (3): 229–250.

Zax, D. (2014), How did computers uncover J. K. Rowling's pseudonym? *Smithsonian.com*, March 2014, Available at: https://www.smithsonianmag.com/science-nature/how-did-computers-uncover-jk-rowlings-pseudonym-180949824/#rIOcjbVb3l8h3VYl.99 (Accessed 21 August 2018).

Zimmerman, D. H. (1998), 'Discoursal identities and social identities', in C. Antaki and S. Widdicombe (eds), *Identities in talk*, 87–106, London: Sage.

Zotzmann, K. and J. P. O'Regan (2016), 'Critical discourse analysis and identity', in *The Routledge handbook of language and identity*, 139–154, London: Routledge.

INDEX